W9-AAY-692

so easy

Electric Guitar

The Ultimate Electric Guitar Course

Method by John McCarthy

Written and adapted by Steve Gorenberg

Supervising Editor: Joe Palombo
Production Manager: Tara Altamuro
Photography: Joe Palombo, Scott Sawala and Paul Enea
Audio Engineer: Jim Rutkowski
Music Transcribing, Engraving and Book Design: Steve Gorenberg

Copy Editors and Proofreaders:
Alex Palombo, Cathy McCarthy and Irene Villaverde

Cover Art Direction and Design:
Paul Enea, Tovero & Marks

ISBN: 978-0-9764347-9-5

Produced by The Rock House Method®

table of contents

about the author

John McCarthy

**creator of the
rock house method**®

John is the creator of **The Rock House Method**®, the world's leading musical instruction system. Over his 20 year career, he has produced and/or appeared in more than 100 instructional products. Millions of people around the world have learned to play music using John's easy to follow, accelerated program.

John is a virtuoso guitarist who has worked with some of the industry's most legendary musicians. He has the ability to break down, teach and communicate music in a manner that motivates and inspires others to achieve their dreams of playing an instrument.

As a guitarist and songwriter, John blends together a unique style of Rock, Metal, Funk and Blues in a collage of melodic compositions, jam-packed with masterful guitar techniques. His sound has been described as a combination of vintage guitar rock with a progressive, gritty edge that is perfectly suited for today's audiences.

Throughout his career, John has recorded and performed with renowned musicians like Doug Wimbish (who has worked with Joe Satriani, Living Colour, The Rolling Stones, Madonna, Annie Lennox and many more top flight artists), Grammy winner Leo Nocentelli, Rock & Roll Hall of Fame inductees Bernie Worrell and Jerome "Big Foot" Brailey, Freekbass, Gary Hoey, Bobby Kimball, David Ellefson (founding member of seven time Grammy nominee Megadeth), Will Calhoun (who has worked with B.B. King, Mick Jagger and Paul Simon), Jordan Giangreco from the acclaimed band The Breakfast, and solo artist Alex Bach. John has also shared the stage with Blue Oyster Cult, Randy Bachman, Marc Rizzo, Jerry Donahue, Bernard Fowler, Stevie Salas, Brian Tichy, Kansas, Al Dimeola and Dee Snyder.

For more information on John, his music and his instructional products visit www.rockhousemethod.com.

introduction

Welcome to **The Rock House Method**® system of learning. You are joining millions of aspiring musicians around the world who use our easy-to-understand methods for learning to play music.

Unlike conventional learning programs, **The Rock House Method**® program is a three-part teaching system that employs CD and 24/7 online lesson support along with this book to give you a variety of sources to assure a complete learning experience. Each product can be used individually or together. The CDs that come with this book match the curriculum exactly, providing you with a live instructor for audio reference. You can pause, rewind, or fast forward any lesson. In addition, the website contains valuable bonus lessons, quizzes and additional rhythms and exercises. The backing tracks that are used throughout this program are included on the CDs. They can also be downloaded from our Lesson Support Site, allowing you to create a custom CD and take your favorite lessons with you anywhere you go.

CREATING MUSICIANS
ONE LESSON AT A TIME

using the lesson support site

Every Rock House product offers FREE membership to our interactive Lesson Support site. Use the member number included with your book to register at www.rockhousemethod.com. Once registered, you will use this fully interactive site along with your product to enhance your learning experience, expand your knowledge, link with instructors, and connect with a community of people around the world who are learning to play music using **The Rock House Method**®. There are sections that directly correspond to this product within the *Additional Information* and *Backing Tracks* sections. There are also a variety of other tools you can utilize such as *Ask The Teacher*, *Quizzes*, *Reference Material*, *Definitions*, *Forums*, *Live Chats*, *Guitar Professor* and much more.

icon key

Throughout this book, you'll periodically notice the following icons. They indicate when there are additional learning tools available on our support website for the section you're working on. When you see an icon in the book, visit the member section of www.rockhousemethod.com for musical backing tracks, additional information and learning utilities.

CD track number

The accompanying CDs include lesson demonstrations, additional information and bass and drum backing tracks. When you see a CD icon and track number, follow along with the included CDs to hear the examples and play along. A complete track listing is also included in the back of this book.

backing track

Many of the exercises in this book are intended to be played along with bass and drum rhythm tracks. This icon indicates that there is a backing track available for download on the Lesson Support Site.

additional information

The question mark icon indicates there is more information for that section available on the website. It can be theory, more playing examples, or tips.

metronome

Metronome icons are placed next to the examples that we recommend you practice using a metronome. You can download a free, adjustable metronome from the support site.

tablature

This icon indicates that there is additional guitar tablature available on the website that corresponds to the lesson. There is also an extensive database of tab music online that is updated regularly.

tuner

Also found on the website is free tuner software which you can download to help you tune your instrument.

Chapter 1
Parts of the Guitar

The guitar is divided into three main sections: the body, the neck and the headstock. The guitar's input jack will be located on the side or front of the body. The assembly that anchors the strings to the body is called the bridge. The saddles hold the strings properly in place; the height of each string (or *action*) can be adjusted with the saddle. Mounted to the body behind the strings are the pickups. A pickup functions like the guitar's microphone; it picks up the vibrations of the strings and converts them to a signal that travels through the guitar cord to the amplifier. Also located on the front of the body are the volume and tone knobs and the pickup selector switch or *toggle switch*. Strap buttons are located on both sides of the body where a guitar strap can be attached. The front face of the neck is called the fretboard (or *fingerboard*). The metal bars going across the fretboard are called frets. The dots are position markers (or *fret markers*) for visual reference to help you gauge where you are on the neck while playing. The nut is the string guide that holds the strings in place where the neck meets the headstock. The headstock contains the machine heads (also referred to as *tuners*); the machine heads are used to tune the strings by tightening or loosening them.

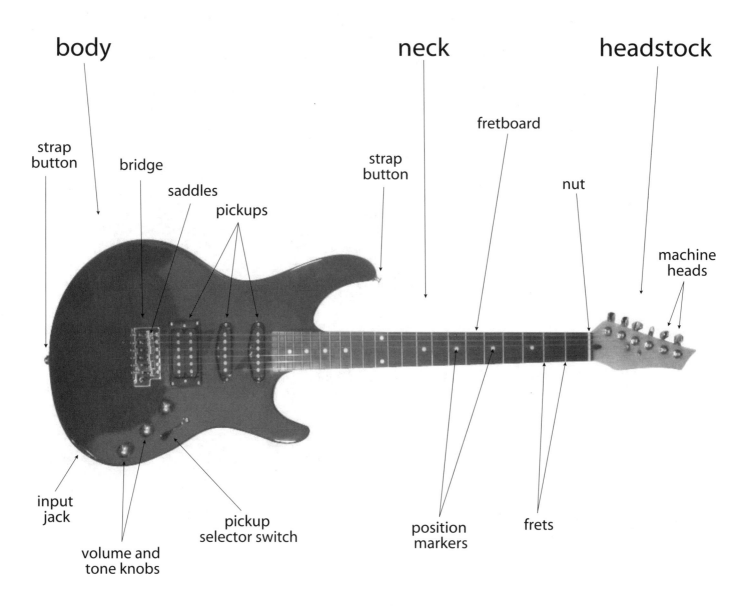

body   neck   headstock

fretboard

strap button   bridge   strap button   nut

saddles

pickups   machine heads

input jack   pickup selector switch   position markers   frets

volume and tone knobs

Holding the Guitar & Pick

Throughout this book, we will refer to the picking hand as your right hand, and the hand fretting the notes as your left hand. If you are left handed and playing a left handed guitar, just make the necessary adjustments as you follow along (read "right hand" to mean your left hand and vice versa).

The photos below show the proper way to hold a guitar. Rest the body of the guitar on your right leg when sitting. When standing, attach a guitar strap to the strap buttons and wear the strap over your left shoulder. Locate the input jack on your guitar. Before you plug in, turn the volume down on the guitar; the amplifier should be *off.* Plug the cord into the guitar and the amplifier, then turn the amp on and bring up the volume.

Rest the guitar on your right leg when seated.

When standing, the guitar strap goes over your left shoulder.

Attach one end of the guitar strap to the top of the body.

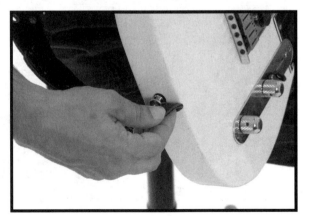

Attach the other end of the strap to the end of the body.

Holding the Pick

Hold the pick between the index finger and thumb of your right hand. Leave just the tip pointing out, perpendicular to your thumb. Your thumb and finger should be placed in the center of the pick, grasping it firmly to give you good control. Leave your hand open (don't make a fist) and let the rest of your fingers hang loosely.

Grasp the pick between your index finger and thumb.

Leave your hand open and your other fingers loose.

To properly position the pick, center the pick on your index finger (Fig. 1) and bring your thumb down on top of it (Fig. 2). Pinch your thumb and finger together and leave just the tip of the pick showing (Fig. 3).

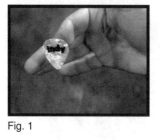

Fig. 1

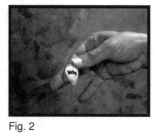

Fig. 2

Fig. 3

Right Hand Position

Place your right arm on the very top of the guitar and let it drape down almost parallel to the bridge (Fig. 4). Leave part of your hand or fingers touching the guitar's body and keep them anchored to the guitar (Fig. 5). This will help give your picking hand a reference point.

Fig. 4

Fig. 5

Left Hand Position

Hold your left hand out in front of you with your wrist straight (Fig. 6). Curl your fingers in and just naturally bring your hand back to the neck of the guitar (Figs. 7 & 8). Try not to bend or contort your wrist. Your fingers should stay curled inward; most of the time only your fingertips will touch the strings when playing. The first joint of your thumb should be in the middle of the back of the neck (Fig. 9). Try to avoid touching the neck with any other part of your hand. Make sure you have the proper right and left hand positions down so that when we progress you'll have no problems.

Fig. 6

Fig. 7

Fig. 8

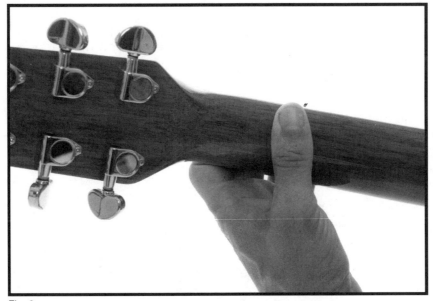
Fig. 9

Names of the Open Strings & Tuning

Each of the six strings on a guitar is tuned to and named after a different note (*pitch*). The thinnest or 1st string is referred to as the highest string because it is the *highest sounding* string. The thickest or 6th string is referred to as the lowest string because it is the *lowest sounding* string. Memorize the names of the open strings. These notes form the basis for finding any other notes on the guitar.

Names of the Open Strings

6th string	5th string	4th string	3rd string	2nd string	1st string
E	A	D	G	B	E

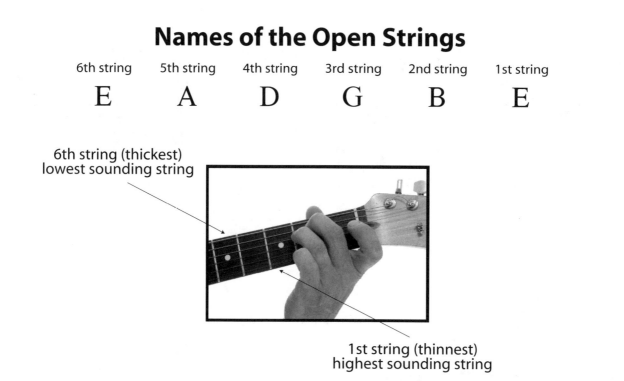

6th string (thickest) lowest sounding string

1st string (thinnest) highest sounding string

Tune your guitar using the machine heads on the headstock. Turn the machine heads a little bit at a time while plucking the string and listening to the change in pitch. Tighten the string to raise the pitch. Loosen the string to lower the pitch. Be careful not to accidentally break a string by tightening it too much or too quickly.

The easiest way to tune a guitar is to use an electronic tuner. There are many different kinds available that are fairly inexpensive. You can also download the free online tuner from www.rockhousemethod.com.

Reading the Chord Chart

5 disc 1

A chord is a group of notes played together. A chord chart (*chord diagram*) is a graphic representation of part of the fretboard (as if you stood the guitar up from floor to ceiling and looked directly at the front of the neck). The vertical lines represent the strings; the horizontal lines represent the frets.

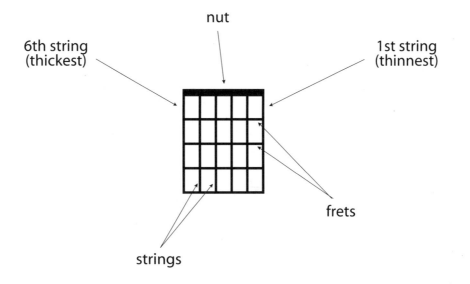

Chord diagrams show which notes to play and which strings they are played on. The solid black dots within the graph represent fretted notes and show you where your fingers should go. Each of these dots will have a number directly below it, underneath the diagram. These numbers indicate which left hand finger to fret the note with (1 = index, 2 = middle, 3 = ring, 4 = pinky). The 0s at the bottom of the diagram show which strings are played open (strummed with no left hand fingers touching them).

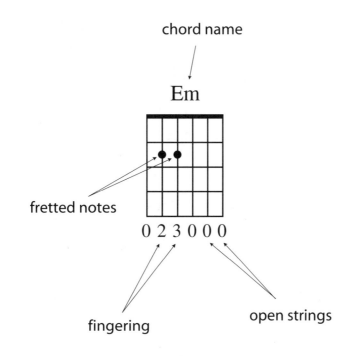

13

Major Open Chords (E - A - D - G)

Our first chords are E major, A major, D major and G major. These are all *open chords* because they either contain open strings or are played in open position (at or near the 1st fret of the guitar). For each chord, the first photo shows what the chord looks like from the front. The second photo is from the player's perspective. Major chords are represented in this book using a capital letter by itself for the chord name. They can also be shown using the letter name followed by a capital letter M, Maj, or Major.

Remember to keep your thumb firmly anchored against the back of the neck. Your fingers should be curled inward toward the fretboard and only the tips of your fingers should be touching the strings. Don't grab the neck with your whole hand; no other parts of your fingers or hand should be touching the neck or any of the other strings. Place your fingertips just to the left of (behind) the fret, pressing the strings inward toward the neck.

E

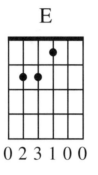

0 2 3 1 0 0

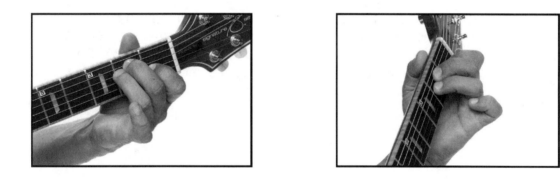

Let's start off with a simple downstrum. Fret the E chord with your left hand. Starting from the 6th string, lightly drag the pick downward across the strings in a smooth motion. The strumming motion should come from your elbow and wrist. When strumming chords, pivot from your elbow and keep your wrist straight. When playing single notes, use more wrist.

One of the hardest things for a beginner to conquer is the ability to play a clean, fully sustained chord without buzzing strings, muted or dead notes. Make sure your left hand is fretting the proper notes and your fingers aren't accidentally touching any of the other strings. Pick each string individually with your right hand, one note at a time. If any of the open strings are deadened or muted, try *slightly* adjusting your fingers. If any of the fretted notes are buzzing, you probably aren't pressing down hard enough with your fingers. It will be difficult at first and might hurt a little, but don't get discouraged. With time and practice, you'll build up callouses on your fingertips. Before you know it, playing chords will be second nature and your fingers will hardly feel it at all.

In the **A** chord diagram, the slur going across the notes means you should *barre* (bar) those notes. A barre is executed by placing one finger flat across more than one string. Pick each note of the chord individually to make sure you're applying enough pressure with your finger. Notice that the 6th and 1st strings each have an "x" below them on the diagram, indicating these strings are not played (either muted or not strummed).

A

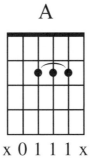

x 0 1 1 1 x

D

x 0 0 1 3 2

G

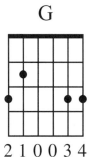

2 1 0 0 3 4

Picking Exercise

Here's an alternate picking exercise to help coordinate your right hand. Instead of strumming the chords, you might pick the notes of a chord out individually and let them ring out together. The following symbols indicate whether a note is picked in an up or a down direction:

⊓ - downpick (pick down toward the floor)   V - uppick (pick up toward the ceiling)

Fret an open D chord and hold the chord shape with your left hand while picking out the individual notes in the order indicated below. This picking pattern (indicated by which number string you pick) is 4 - 1 - 3 - 1 - 2 - 1. Recite the string number while you pick each one to help memorize the order. Use a down-up-down-up alternate picking pattern. Notice that the 1st string is always uppicked, while the other strings are all downpicked. Try to hold one of your right hand fingers on the body of the guitar to help give you added support and control. Practice playing in a steady, even rhythm, in time with a metronome.

D

x 0 0 1 3 2

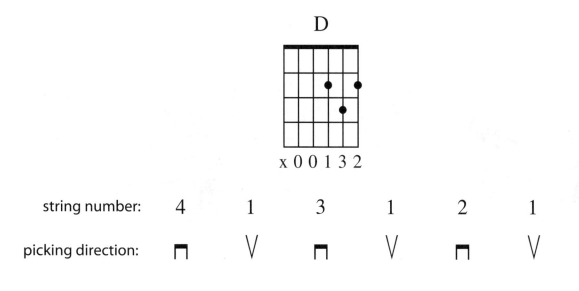

string number:	4	1	3	1	2	1
picking direction:	⊓	V	⊓	V	⊓	V

Chord Progressions

Once you have the chords sounding clean and the strumming motion down the next step is to learn how to change chords quickly and cleanly. Focus on where each finger needs to move for the next chord. Sometimes one or more of your fingers will be able to stay in the same place. Avoid taking your hand completely off the neck. Instead, try to move your whole hand as little as possible and make smaller finger adjustments to change from one chord to the next. When you can change from chord to chord seamlessly, you'll be able to play complete songs.

The following is an example of a *chord progression* and is written on a musical *staff*. A staff is the group of horizontal lines on which music is written. The chord names above the staff show which chord to play, and the *rhythm slashes* indicate the rhythm in which the chords are strummed. A chord progression is a series of chords played in a specified rhythm and order. In this chord progression, strum each chord eight times, using all downstrums. This example also uses *repeat signs* (play through the progression and repeat it again). Listen and play along with the backing track to hear how it should sound. Keep practicing and try to change chords in time without stalling or missing a beat. Count along out loud with each strum, in time and on the beat. Start out slowly if you need to and gradually get it up to speed.

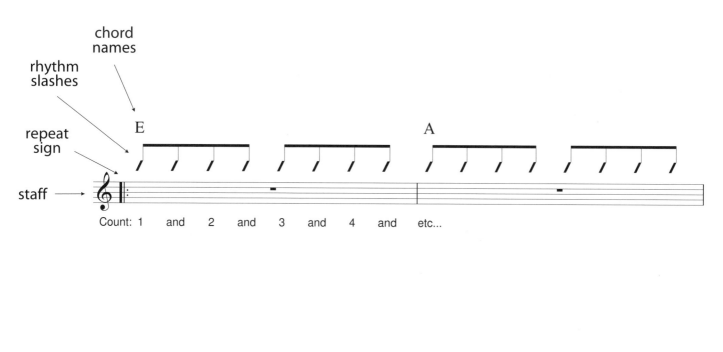

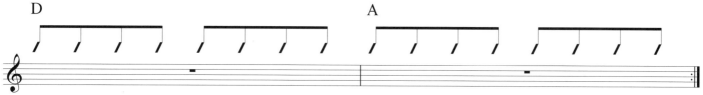

Rhythm Notation

You don't need to read traditional music notation in order to play guitar, but it's helpful to understand a little bit about the concept of rhythm and timing. In most popular rock and blues, music is divided into *measures* of four beats. When a band counts off "One, two, three, four" at the beginning of a song, it represents one complete measure of music. Different types of notes are held for different durations within a measure. For example, a *quarter note* gets one beat because a quarter note is held for one quarter of a measure.

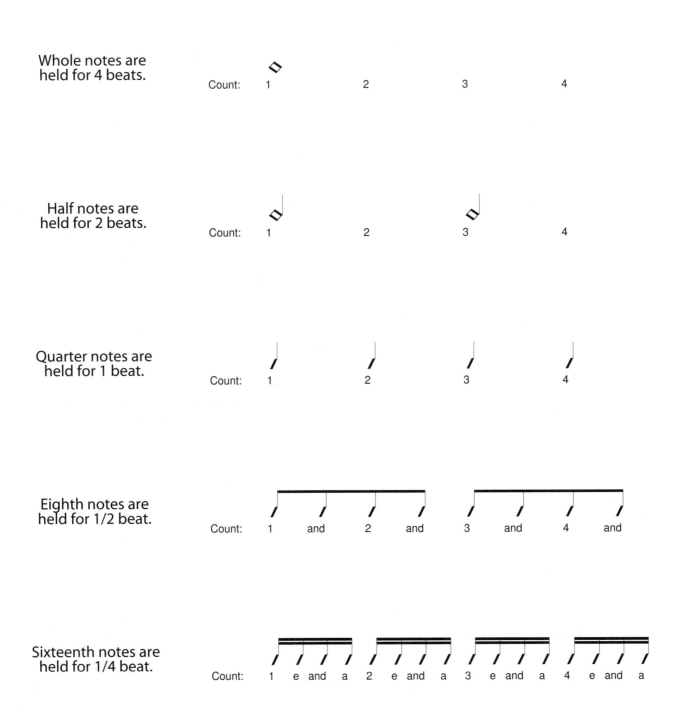

Whole notes are held for 4 beats.
Count: 1   2   3   4

Half notes are held for 2 beats.
Count: 1   2   3   4

Quarter notes are held for 1 beat.
Count: 1   2   3   4

Eighth notes are held for 1/2 beat.
Count: 1   and   2   and   3   and   4   and

Sixteenth notes are held for 1/4 beat.
Count: 1 e and a 2 e and a 3 e and a 4 e and a

A *tie* is a curved line connecting one note to the next. If two notes are tied, strike only the first one and let it ring out through the duration of the second note (or "tied" note).

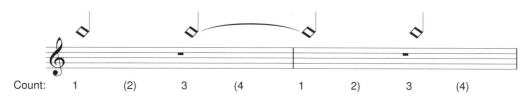

Count: 1   (2)   3   (4)   1   2)   3   (4)

A *dot* after a note increases its value by another 1/2 of its original value. In the following example the half notes are dotted, so they are held for three beats.

Count: 1   (2   3)   4   1   (2   3)   4

Reading Tablature

Tablature (or *tab*) is a number system for reading notes on the neck of a guitar. It does not require you to have knowledge of standard music notation. This system was designed specifically for the guitar. Most music for guitar is available in tab. Tablature is a crucial and essential part of your guitar playing career.

The six lines of the tablature staff represent each of the six strings. The top line is the thinnest (highest pitched) string. The bottom line is the thickest (lowest pitched) string. The lines in between are the 2nd through 5th strings. The numbers placed directly on these lines show you the fret number to play the note at. At the bottom, underneath the staff, is a series of numbers. These numbers show you which left hand fingers you should use to fret the notes.

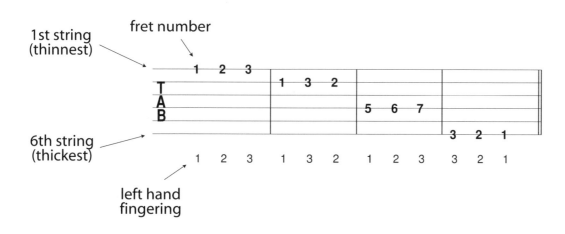

Chords can also be written in tab. If there are several numbers stacked together in a column, those notes should be played or strummed at the same time. Here are the four open major chords you already know from the previous section with the tablature written out underneath each diagram. Since the fingerings are shown on the chord diagrams, we won't bother to repeat them underneath the tab.

E

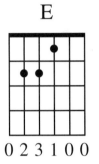

0 2 3 1 0 0

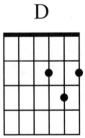

A

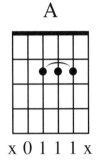

x 0 1 1 1 x

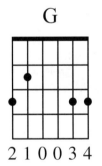

D

x 0 0 1 3 2

G

2 1 0 0 3 4

Chapter 2

Finger Exercise

This is a finger exercise in tablature that will build coordination and strengthen your fingers. It's designed to help stretch your hand out, so keep your fingers spread out across the four frets, one finger per fret. Leave your first finger anchored in place and reach for the following three notes by stretching your hand out.

With your right hand, use alternate picking in a consistent down-up-down-up pendulum motion. Alternate picking will help develop speed, smoothness and technique. Practice this exercise using the metronome for timing and control.

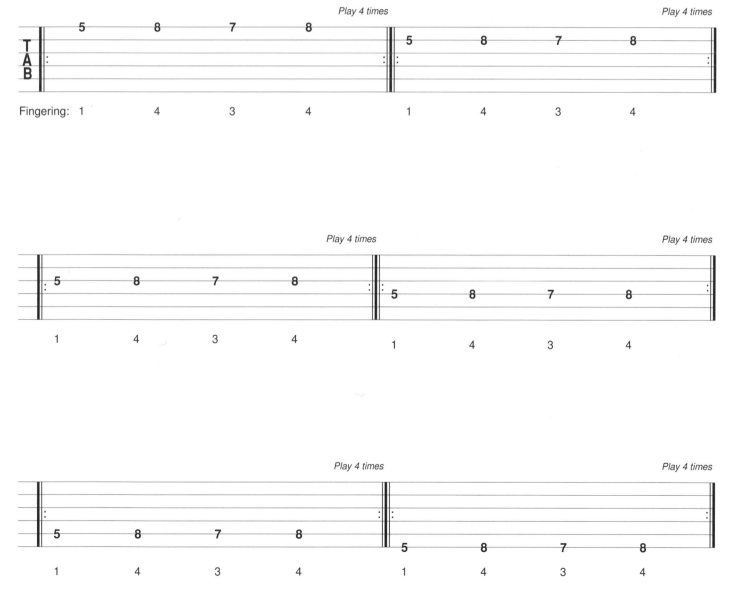

Blues Rhythm

The following is a basic blues riff in the key of A. This riff is made up of two note chords shown on the tab staff. The chord names above the staff are there as a reference to show you what the basic harmony is while you play along.

This riff should sound very familiar - it's used more than any other blues progression. Plenty of rock and blues classics are played entirely with this one riff repeated over and over. It is made up of twelve measures (or *bars*) of music called the *12-bar blues*, a blues progression consisting of twelve repeated bars of music.

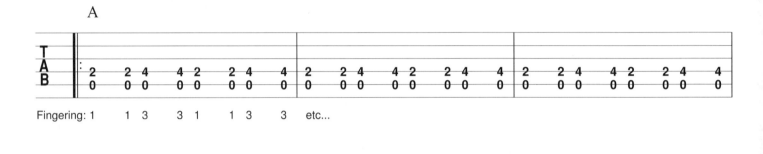

Fingering: 1   1 3   3 1   1 3   3   etc...

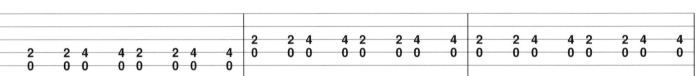

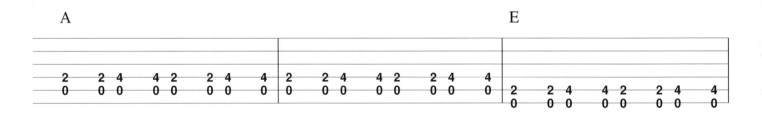

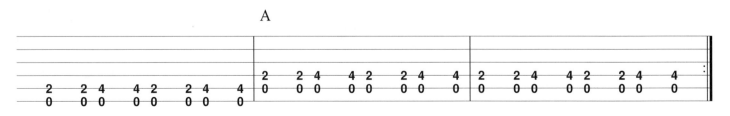

Blues is played with a *shuffle feel*, also called a triplet feel. This example was written in eighth notes and the second eighth note of each beat should lag a little. This is referred to as triplet feel because the beat is actually divided by thirds, counted as if there were three eighth notes per beat instead of two. The first part of the beat gets 2/3 of a beat and the second part only gets 1/3.

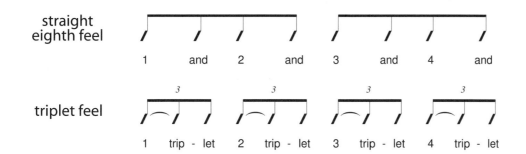

Shuffle feel is a much easier concept to understand by hearing it. Listen to the backing track, count along and try to get the triplet feel in your head. Also, check out almost any blues standard, slow or fast and you'll probably recognize a shuffle feel being used.

This 12-bar blues riff is also an example of a **I - IV - V** (one - four - five) chord progression. The Roman numerals refer to the steps of the scale, relative to what key the music is in. This blues riff is in the key of A, so the A chord is the **I** chord (also called the *tonic*). The D chord is the **IV** chord (also called the *subdominant*) because in the key of A, D is the fourth step of the scale. Finally, the **V** chord (or *dominant*) is the E chord, because E is the fifth step of the scale in the key of A.

The I - IV - V chord progression is the most common progression used in rock or blues. It's the foundation that all rock and blues was built on and has evolved from. There are many variations, but songs such as "Johnny B. Goode," "You Really Got Me," "Rock and Roll," "I Love Rock and Roll" and "Sympathy for the Devil" are all based on the I - IV - V.

Rock Riffs

A riff is a repeated musical phrase made up of a series of single notes. Many rock songs are based upon one or two simple riffs. Below are two rock riff examples designed to help coordinate your right and left hands together. The first riff is in a heavy metal style, the second has a fast blues feel. Try using all downpicking for the first riff to get that aggressive, heavy metal sound. The second riff is played using a combination of downpicking and alternate picking; follow the picking symbols above the staff to improve your rhythm and accuracy.

Rock Riff #1

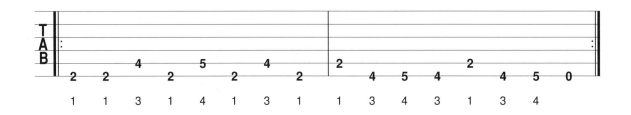

Rock Riff #2

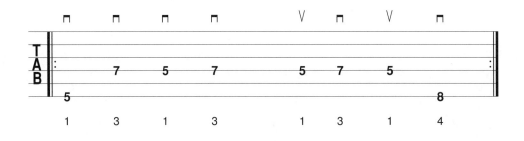

Minor Open Chords (Am - Em - Dm)

18
disc 1

Here are the three most popular minor open chords: **Am**, **Em**, and **Dm**. Minor chords have a sad or melancholy sound, whereas major chords have a happy or bright sound. A lowercase "m" within a chord name indicates a minor chord.

Am

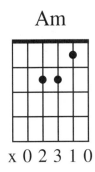

x 0 2 3 1 0

Am

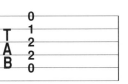

```
    0
  T 1
  A 2
  B 2
    0
```

Em

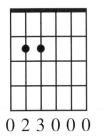

0 2 3 0 0 0

Em

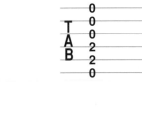

```
    0
  T 0
  A 0
  B 2
    2
    0
```

Here's an alternate fingering for the Em chord using the first and second fingers. Depending on the context in which it's used in a chord progression, it might be easier to change from chord to chord by slightly varying the fingering. Both fingerings of the chord are useful to know.

Em

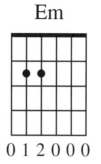

0 1 2 0 0 0

Dm

0 1 2 0 0 0

Dm

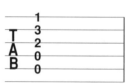

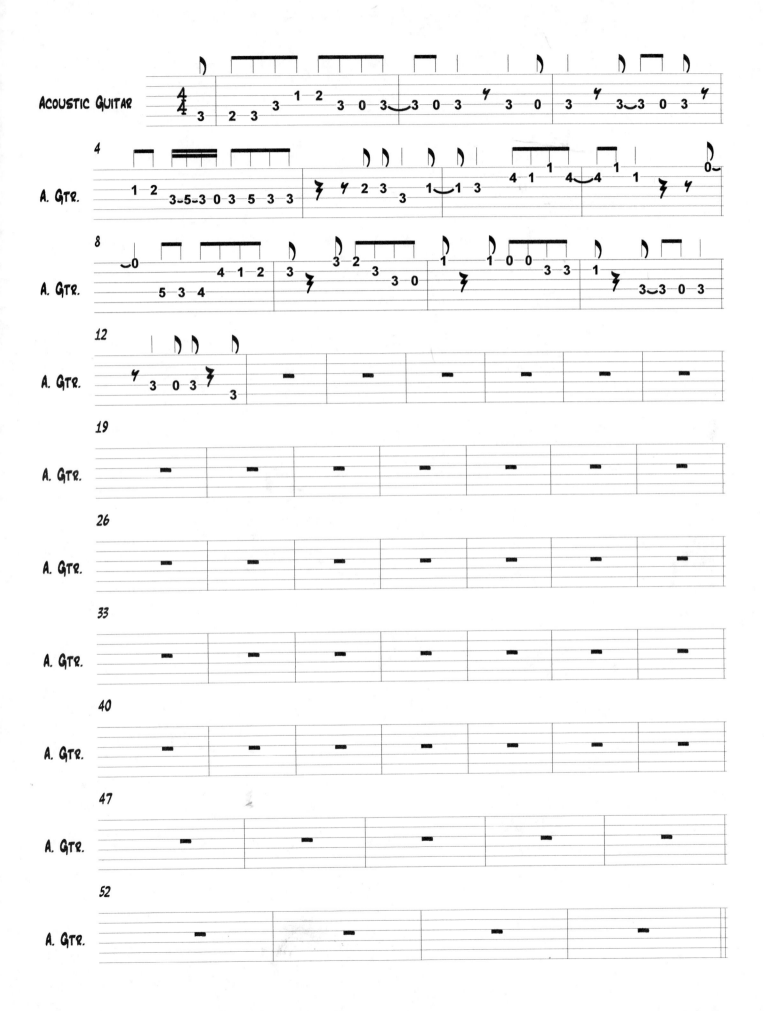

Autumn Leaves

ii^{mi7} V^7 I^{MA7} IV^{MA7}

Dmi^7 G^7 C^{MA7} F^{MA7}

$vii^°$ III^7 vi vi

$B^{°7}$ E^7 Ami^7 Ami^7

36.

36.

AUTUMN LEAVES — JOHNNY MERCER

(MED. JAZZ)

BILL EVANS — "PORTRAIT IN JAZZ"

Major & Minor Chord Rhythm

This chord progression combines both major and minor chords in the key of A minor. The four chords used in the progression are shown in order using chord diagrams below. Use the alternate fingering for the Em chord (with your first and second fingers) to make changing from chord to chord easier. Notice how similar the fingerings are between the Am and C chords; simply move your third finger and leave your other fingers stationary. Play along with the backing track and practice changing chords cleanly and in time. Use the strumming pattern indicated by the symbols above the tab staff.

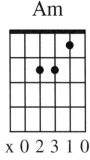

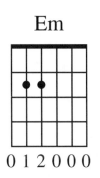

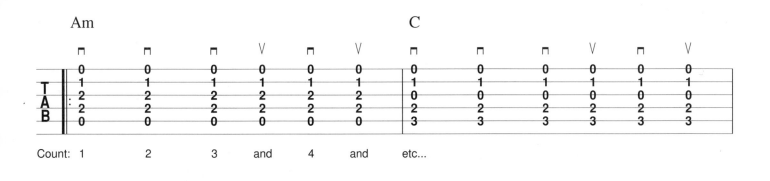

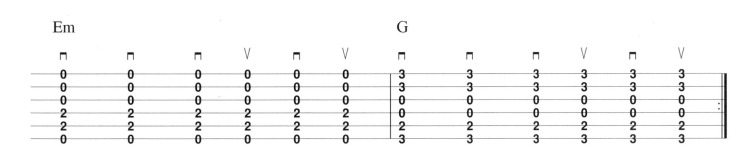

27

Minor Pentatonic Scales

Minor pentatonic scales are the most commonly used scales for playing rock and blues solos. The pentatonic is a five note scale, or an abbreviated version of the full natural minor scale. The word "pentatonic" comes from the greek words, "penta" (five) and "tonic" (the keynote).

Here is the A minor pentatonic scale shown in tab. Practice the scale ascending and descending using consistent alternate picking. Memorize this scale; it's the one you'll use most often for playing melodies and leads.

1st Position A Minor Pentatonic Scale (Ascending)

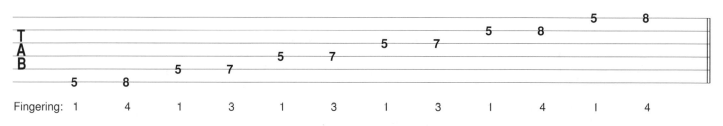

Fingering: 1   4   1   3   1   3   I   3   I   4   I   4

1st Position A Minor Pentatonic Scale (Descending)

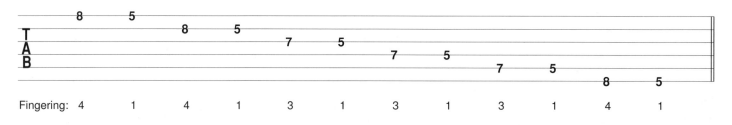

Fingering: 4   1   4   1   3   1   3   1   3   1   4   1

Scale Diagrams

Scale diagrams are similar to the chord diagrams you've already seen. A scale diagram shows all the notes in the scale within a certain position on the neck. This diagram is for the 1st position A minor pentatonic scale you've just learned. The stacked numbers below indicate the fingering for the notes on each string.

1st position
A minor pentatonic scale

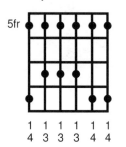

There are five different positions of the minor pentatonic scale, each beginning on a different note of the scale. Once you've learned all five positions, you'll be able to play leads using this scale anywhere on the neck.

Here is the 2nd position minor pentatonic scale, beginning at the 8th fret on the second note of the scale. Once you've got the first two positions of the minor pentatonic scale mastered, you can log on to www.rockhousemethod.com and get the other three positions.

2nd Position A Minor Pentatonic Scale (Ascending)

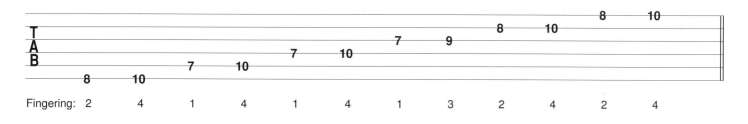

Fingering: 2   4   1   4   1   4   1   3   2   4   2   4

2nd Position A Minor Pentatonic Scale (Descending)

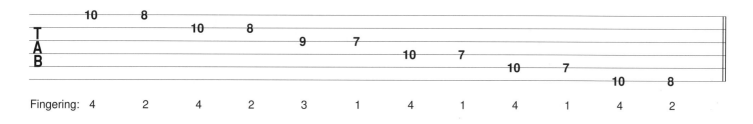

Fingering: 4   2   4   2   3   1   4   1   4   1   4   2

2nd position
A minor pentatonic scale

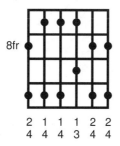

8fr

2 1 1 1 2 2
4 4 4 3 4 4

Triplet Lead Pattern

The following examples are standard lead pattern exercises, designed to help you build coordination and learn how to begin using the minor pentatonics for playing leads. Use alternate picking and the metronome to start out slowly and get the rhythm. Memorize the patterns and gradually speed up the tempo. Before you know it, you'll be playing blazing rock and metal guitar solos.

1st Position Triplet Lead Pattern

Here is the 1st position A minor pentatonic scale played in groups of three notes, or triplets. A triplet is a group of three equal notes played within one beat. Count "one - two - three, one - two - three" or "one trip-let, two trip-let" out loud while you play through this exercise to get the triplet feel in your head.

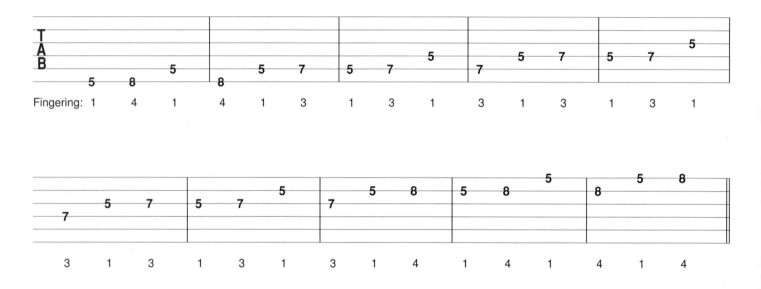

Now let's play the same pattern in reverse, back down the scale in triplets.

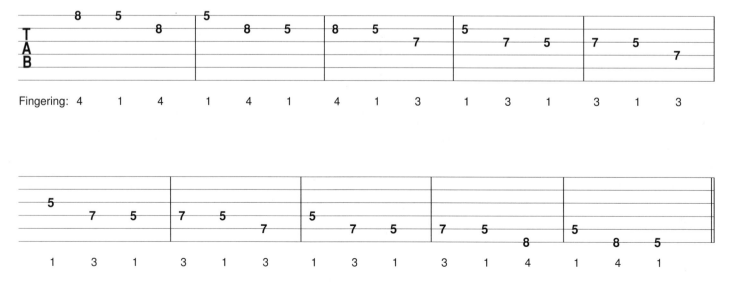

2nd Position Triplet Lead Pattern

You can use the triplet pattern to practice all of your scales and make it part of your warmup routine. Here is the 2nd position A minor pentatonic scale played ascending and descending using the same triplet pattern. Practice using consistent alternate picking to build speed and achieve a clean, smooth tone.

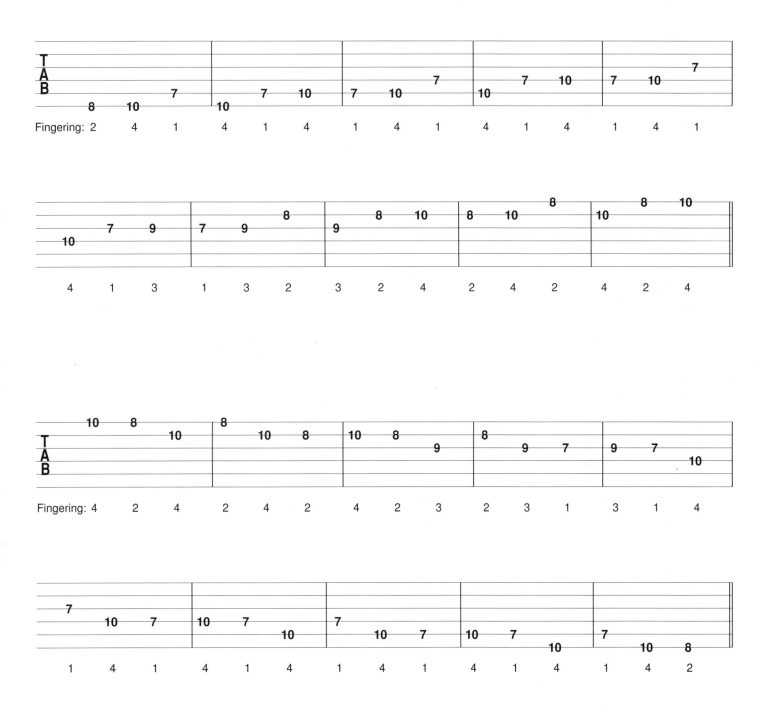

Lead Techniques: Bending

Bending

Now let's learn some lead guitar techniques that will add expression to your playing. Bends are a very soulful way of creating emotion with the guitar, using flesh against steel to alter and control pitches. All guitarists have their own unique, signature way of bending notes.

The row of tab staffs below shows bends using the third, fourth or first fingers. The "B" above the staff indicates a bend, and the arrow with a "1" above it means to bend the note one whole step in pitch.

First try the third finger bend. While fretting the note with your third finger, keep your first two fingers down on the string behind it and push upward using all three fingers. This will give you added coordination and control. Use the same technique for the fourth finger bend, using all four fingers to bend the string upward. The first finger bend will probably be the hardest since you are only using one finger to bend the string. In some situations, you may even pull the string downward with your first finger to bend the note. If you want to check the pitch of your bend, first play the note two frets higher from the note you are going to bend. This should be the pitch you want to bend the note up to.

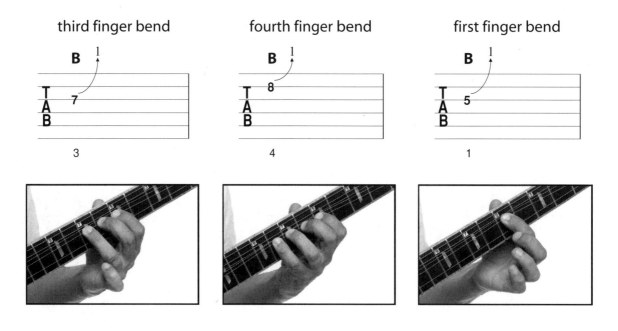

The following example shows what the bends might look like in context when playing a solo in the 1st position A minor pentatonic scale. Play through this exercise and start to get a feel for how to incorporate bends into your own riffs.

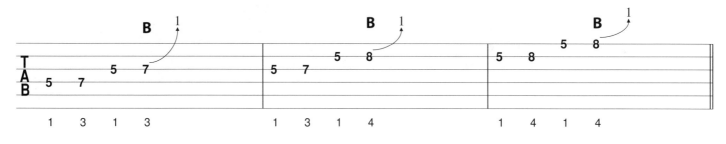

Lead Techniques:
Hammer Ons & Pull Offs

Hammer Ons

A hammer on is also a widely used lead technique. On the staff below, you'll see a slur connecting one tab number to the next. This indicates that only the first tab number is picked; the second note is not struck. The "H" above the slur indicates a hammer on.

To play a hammer on, pick the first note and then push down the next note using just your left hand finger (without picking it). Play through the following series of hammer ons below to see how you can use these with the minor pentatonic scale.

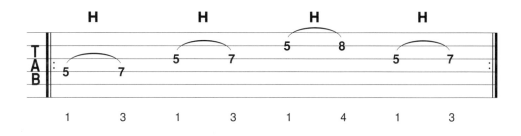

Pull Offs

Pull offs are the opposite of hammer ons. Pick the first note and pull or snap your finger off the string to get the second note. Your first finger should already be in place, fretting the second note in advance. The "P" above each slur below indicates a pull off.

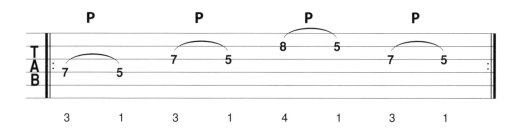

Blues Lead

Here's an example of a solo that can be played over the Blues Rhythm you learned earlier. This solo incorporates bends, hammer ons and pull offs in a variety of positions. The riff in the first measure is one of the most commonly used blues riffs; it can be heard in countless blues guitar solos. After you've got this solo down, try to create your own using all of the lead techniques and positions of the A minor pentatonic scales.

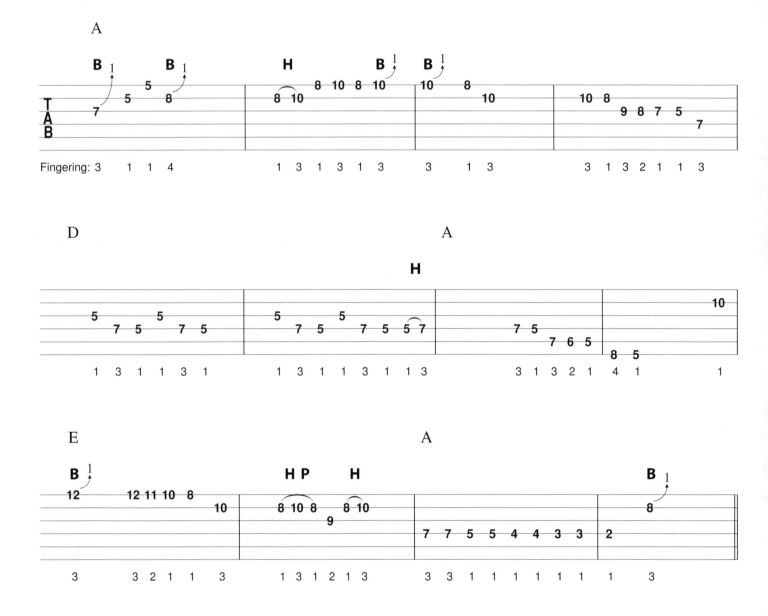

end of chapter 2

Before you continue to the next section, use your member number and log on to www.rockhousemethod.com to visit our online community. Review the additional information, take a quiz and test your knowledge of open chords, tablature, blues rhythms, minor pentatonic scales and lead techniques. See you in the next section!

Chapter 3

Power Chords

30-31
disc 1

Power chords are simple two note chords that are used extensively in rock and metal. Power chords sound their fullest and heaviest when played with distortion. Below are two power chords shown at the 1st fret; both are played using just the first and third fingers.

F5

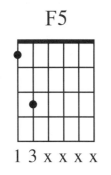

1 3 x x x x

F5

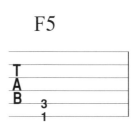

B♭5

x 1 3 x x x

B♭5

The two notes that make up power chords (also referred to as *five* chords) are called the *root note* and the *fifth*. The root note of the F5 power chord is F, the note that gives the chord its name. The other note is a C, which is the fifth note up the musical alphabet from the root note (F-G-A-B-C). These power chords are actually abbreviated versions of regular major and minor chords. Major and minor chords are made up of root notes, thirds and fifths. The third is the note which determines whether a chord is major or minor. Since power chords contain no thirds, they are neither major nor minor. Because of this, power chords can be an ideal choice for many different keys and styles.

Power chords are *moveable* chords; if you move the same fingering to another fret, the name of the chord changes. This is called *transposing* the chord. Notice that the lowest note of each power chord is the root note. Using the musical alphabet and the chromatic scale, you can transpose the power chords to any chord in the scale. For example, if you take the F5 chord and move it one whole step higher to the third fret, it will become a G5 power chord. The chart below shows the notes along the fifth and sixth strings up to the 12th fret. You can use this chart to transpose the F5 and B♭5 power chords to any other fret.

6th string notes (F5 chord)	E	F	F♯	G	G♯	A	A♯	B	C	C♯	D	D♯	E
fret number	Open	1	2	3	4	5	6	7	8	9	10	11	12
5th string notes (B♭5 chord)	A	B♭	B	C	C♯	D	D♯	E	F	F♯	G	G♯	A

Power Chord Progression

Here's a popular progression using all power chords. Use only your first and third fingers to fret each chord and practice moving smoothly from chord to chord. This exercise has been written in eighth notes, but you can experiment with the rhythm and strumming and come up with your own variations. Play along with the backing track and try it in different ways. Instead of eighth notes, try playing sixteenth notes, quarter notes or half notes. You can use alternate strumming, or try using all downstrums to create a chunkier, metal sound. As you progress, you'll notice that the way you attack or strum the strings will make a big difference in the overall sound.

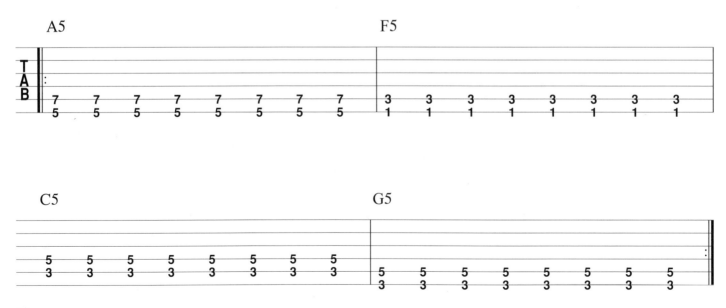

More Power Chord Rhythms

Here are some more fun power chord rhythms to practice. Most heavy metal rhythms like these sound best using all downpicking to get that thick metal tone. Crank up the distortion and get your metal horns up!

Power Chord Rhythm #1

The first example uses the 5th string power chords E5, C5 and D5. This is a very popular chord progression in E minor and is used in many metal songs. The rhythm count is indicated under the staff to help you master the timing.

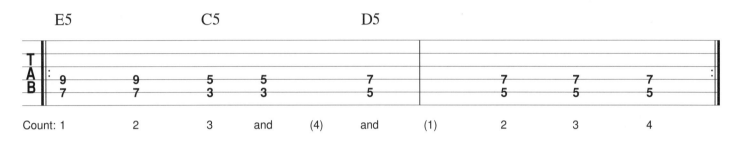

Power Chord Rhythm #2

This rhythm uses two 6th string power chords and has an example of a technique called *palm muting*. Mute the strings slightly with the side of your picking hand close to the bridge while downstrumming. Avoid deadening the notes completely by just lightly touching the strings to get the muting effect. The P.M. symbol followed by a dashed line over beats 3 and 4 show which chords to palm mute. The first two beats should not be muted.

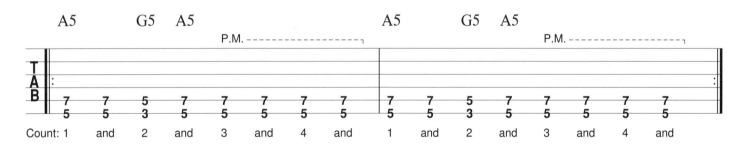

Power Chord Rhythm #3

The last rhythm mixes 5th and 6th string power chords in the key of Em. This is another popular and powerful metal chord change. Count out loud and play along to get the rhythm down.

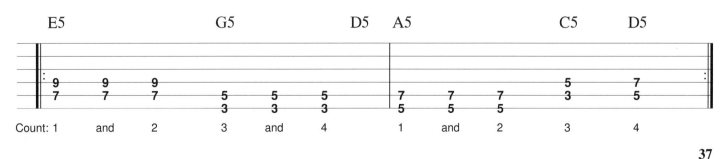

Barre Chords

Two very important chords are the F and B♭ barre chords. These are full barre chords containing no open strings, so they are moveable chords that can be transposed to any fret.

Full barre chords are especially difficult to play. For the F barre chord, you need to barre your first finger across all six strings, then add the other three notes as well. Pick out each note individually to make sure it sounds clean and you've got it down. After mastering these chords, you'll be able to play in any key and position on the guitar.

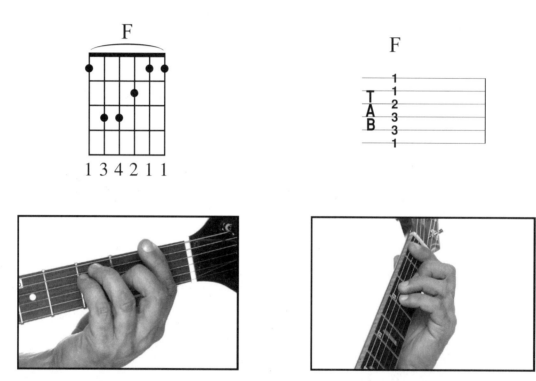

Use the same chromatic scale chart from the Power Chords section to transpose any of the barre chords in this lesson. Notice that the lowest two notes of each chord are the same notes that make up the power chords. Power chords are just simple abbreviations of the regular full barre chords. You can use either the full barre chords or the power chords to change the sound or texture of a rhythm. By just varying how many strings you pick, you can easily incorporate both versions of the chord within a progression. This is another great trick to use in developing your own unique strumming style.

6th string notes (F chord)	E	F	F♯	G	G♯	A	A♯	B	C	C♯	D	D♯	E
fret number	Open	1	2	3	4	5	6	7	8	9	10	11	12
5th string notes (B♭ chord)	A	B♭	B	C	C♯	D	D♯	E	F	F♯	G	G♯	A

For the B♭ chord, you need to barre across three strings with your third finger. The Fm and B♭m chords are only slightly different. All of these chords are also moveable using the chart.

B♭

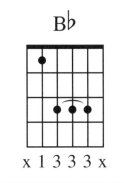

x 1 3 3 3 x

B♭

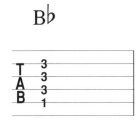

```
T   3
A   3
    3
B   1
```

Fm

1 3 4 1 1 1

Fm

```
    1
T   1
A   1
    3
B   3
    1
```

B♭m

x 1 3 4 2 1

B♭m

```
    1
T   2
A   3
    3
B   1
```

The F7 and B♭7 barre chords are both played using a first finger barre. They are *dominant seventh* chords and have a colorful blues tone. These chords are often used as substitutes for regular major chords when playing blues songs.

F7

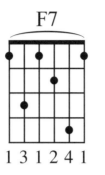

1 3 1 2 4 1

F7

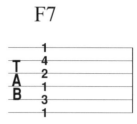

```
     1
T    4
     2
A    1
B    3
     1
```

B♭7

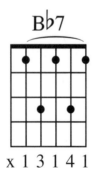

x 1 3 1 4 1

B♭7

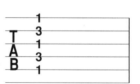

```
     1
T    3
     1
A    3
B    1
```

Rock Rhythm

This is a very popular rock progression in the key of A minor that uses all barre chords. Since all of the chords are moveable chords, you can transpose this entire progression to any other key. The four chords used in this key are shown in the chord diagrams below. The rhythm is straight eighth notes and should be played using all downstrums to get that heavy rock feel. Play along with the CD or download the backing track from the Lesson Support Site and practice playing along.

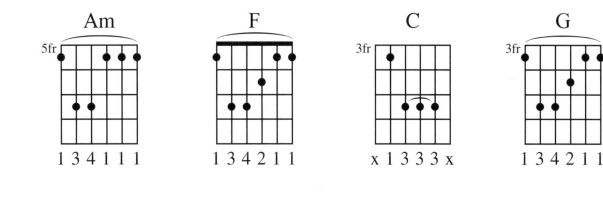

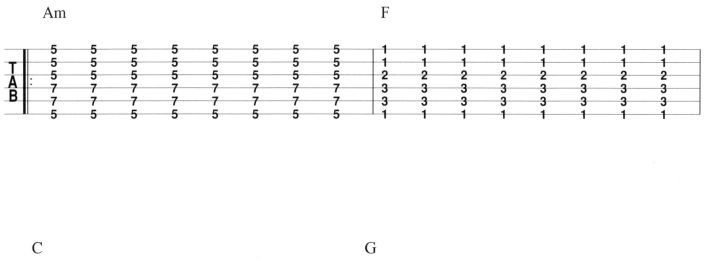

Rock Lead

Here's a rock lead using the A minor pentatonic scales that you can play over the rock rhythm you've just learned. The chord names are shown above the staff for a reference. This is an example of how to use the different positions of the minor pentatonic scales, bends, hammer ons and pull offs to play rock solos.

The lead starts off in the 1st position and moves up to the 2nd position on the second staff. The top of the next page shows a hammer on and pull off pattern similar to the lead pattern shown earlier in this section. Go through each riff slowly along with the CD and when you're ready, try playing in time with the backing track.

Once you've got it, try coming up with your own lead. All five positions of the A minor pentatonic scale can be found at www.rockhousemethod.com. Learn how to switch smoothly from one position to the next, and soon you'll be able to play blazing rock solos anywhere on the fretboard.

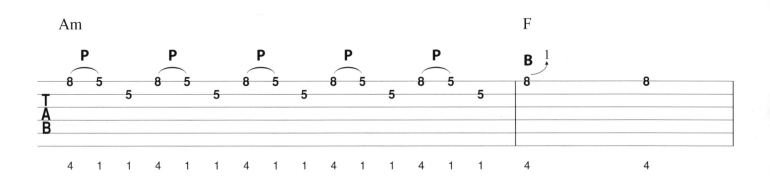

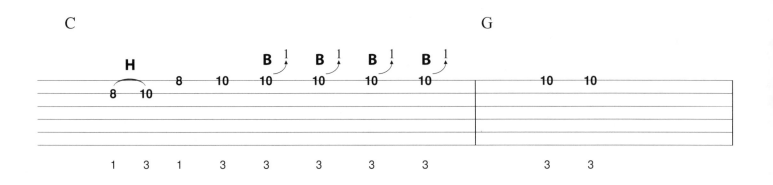

42

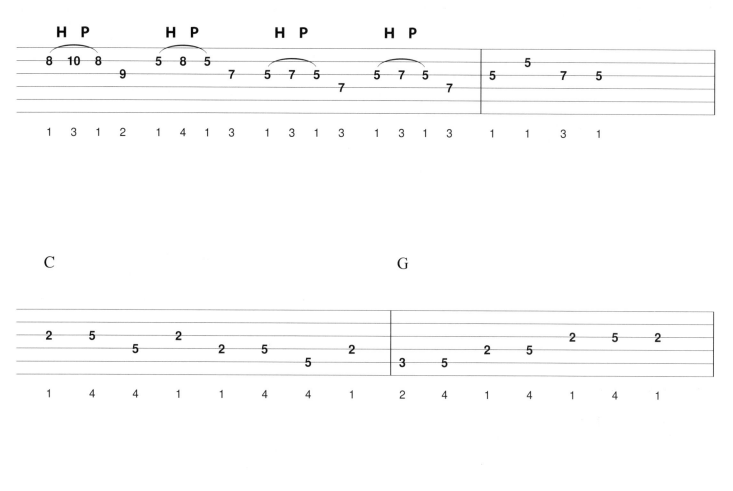

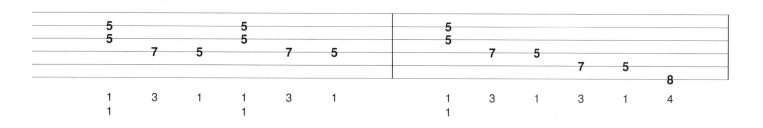

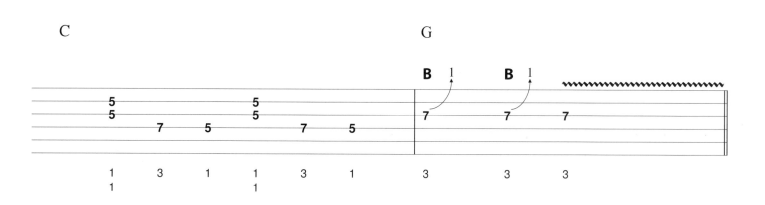

Changing the Feel of a Song

By altering the strumming or picking pattern of a chord progression, you can dramatically change the style. In this section, we'll show you how to take the simple chord progression from the previous lesson, change the rhythm and use it to play many different genres of music, all against the same bass and drum backing track. This demonstrates the power of the guitar and its ability to dictate the feel of the song. Since all of the chords are moveable chords, you can also transpose this entire progression to any other key.

Metal

To play the chord progression with a metal feel, just double up on your strumming and play the figure using all sixteenth notes.

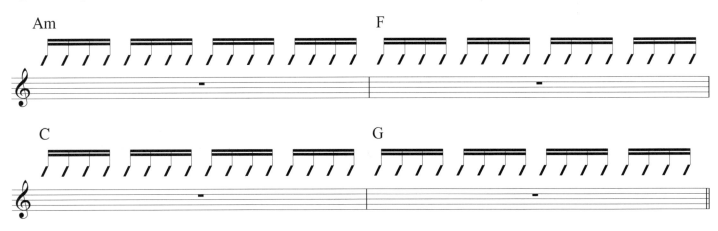

Reggae

Reggae uses all upstrokes. Following each upstrum of the pick, mute the strings with your picking hand in time and on the downbeat to give it that reggae feel.

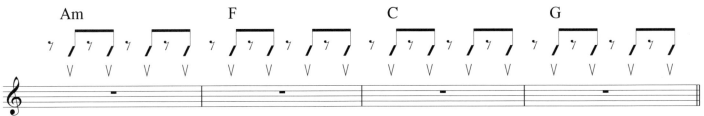

Count: (1) and (2) and (3) and (4) and (etc.)

Ballad

This is a rock ballad picking pattern. Fret and hold each barre chord, and downpick the notes individually. Let the notes ring out together for the duration of each measure.

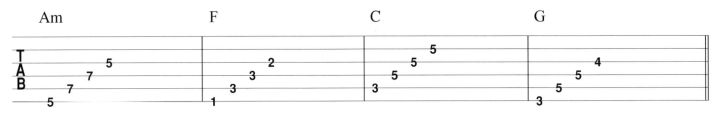

Drop D Tuning
Metal Rhythm

Drop D tuning refers to lowering the pitch of the 6th string from E to D. This gives the guitar a heavier, meaner sound. Drop D has been used for years in hard rock and heavy metal, so much so that many bands have written their entire catalogs in Drop D.

To tune your guitar to Drop D tuning, strike the open 4th string (D) and the open 6th string together and gradually lower the 6th string from E to D until the 4th and 6th strings sound "in tune" with each other. These two strings are now both tuned to D an octave apart from each other. You can check your tuning using the online tuner at www.rockhousemethod.com to make sure you've got it.

Drop D is extremely easy to play in because the 6th string power chords are now played with just one finger. Simply barre one finger across the lowest two or three strings at any fret. You can also play a D5 chord just by strumming the lowest two or three open strings. Below are three chord diagrams to give you some ideas on how to use Drop D tuning to play chords.

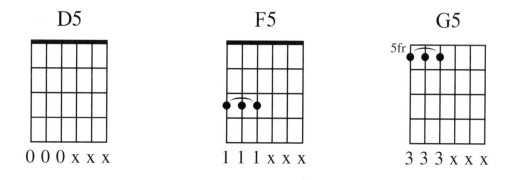

The following rhythm is a popular heavy metal style riff in Drop D tuning. Pay attention to the picking symbols to get that chunky, heavy metal feel. Try muting the strings by lightly resting the heel of your right hand against the strings. After you've got this one, experiment with your own riffs in Drop D tuning.

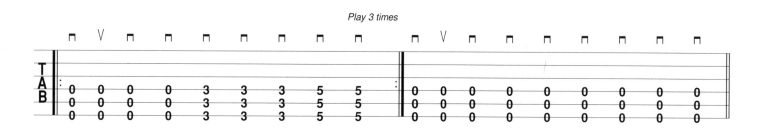

The C Major Scale

The major scale is the foundation of all other scales and chords. If you count up from C to C using the musical alphabet (C - D - E - F - G - A - B - C), you will have a C major scale. The first note of the scale is C (also known as the *root note*). The root note gives a scale, key or chord its name. The distance (in pitch) from the first C to the next higher or lower C in the musical alphabet is called an *octave*. Major scales contain seven different name notes. In this section we'll cover five positions of the C major scale, beginning with a review of the 1st position scale from Learn Rock Acoustic Beginner. This is a two octave scale, since you can play through two full octaves of the scale in this position. It is also called the 1st position major scale, because the first note played in this position is the root note C. For each scale position, the root notes (all of the C's) are circled on the tab staff. In the scale diagrams to the right, the root notes are indicated with open circles. Knowing the placement of the root notes is important for playing solos.

1st Position C Major Scale

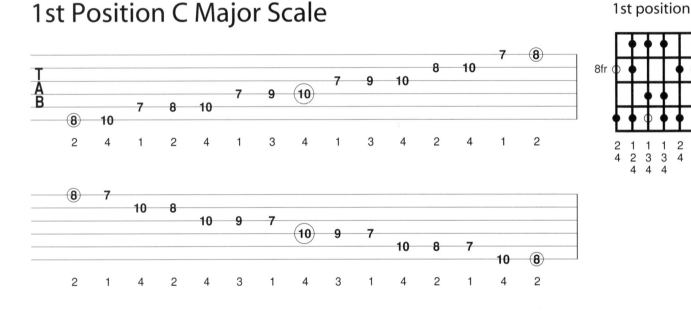

Half Steps & Whole Steps

The distance in pitch between any two musical notes is called an *interval*. An interval is how much higher or lower one note sounds from another, or the space in between the notes. The smallest interval on the guitar is from a fretted note to the fret next to it on the same string. This distance is called a *half step*. Twice the distance, or the distance of two frets, is called a *whole step*.

The musical alphabet uses the letters **A** through **G**. The distance from one letter or note to the next is usually a whole step (two frets), with two exceptions: there is only a half step between the notes **B** and **C** and between the notes **E** and **F**.

	whole step	half step	whole step	whole step	half step	whole step	whole step	
A		B		C	D		E	F	G	A

After counting up from **A** to **G**, we get to a higher sounding **A** and can continue to count up higher through the alphabet again from there. The distance from that first **A** to the next **A** is an octave.

The Chromatic Scale

Counting up or down the musical alphabet in half steps (or frets) is called a chromatic scale. The regular letters of the alphabet are called *natural notes*. Where there is a whole step between two natural notes, the note that falls in between them is a *sharp* (♯) or *flat* (♭) note. The ♯ next to a note makes the note a half step higher. The ♭ lowers the note a half step. For example, the note in between A and B can be called either an A♯ or a B♭, since it's actually the same note with two different names. Whether you call a note sharp or flat depends on what key you're playing in or what the context is. The half steps that occur between B and C and between E and F (where there aren't other notes between them), are referred to as *natural half steps*. If you memorize where these two natural half steps occur, you can use that knowledge to find any note on the guitar. Just start with any open string and count up in half steps.

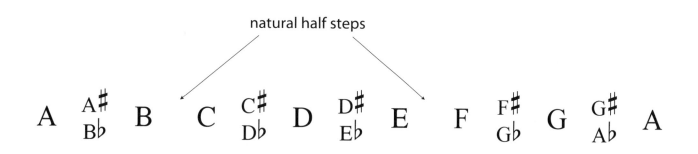

Intervals of the Major Scale

The sequence of whole steps and half steps is what gives a scale or key its *tonality*. There is a specific sequence of intervals for a major scale, and this formula is the same no matter what key the major scale is in. In the chart below, you can see that within the major scale, the half steps fall between the 3rd and 4th steps, and between the 7th and the octave. All of the other intervals are whole steps. This will be true for any major scale. All together in order, the sequence of intervals (steps) for a major scale are whole - whole - half - whole - whole - whole - half. Scale steps are numbered using roman numerals. The tonic, subdominant, and dominant (I - IV - V) are capitalized because they represent the major chords in the key.

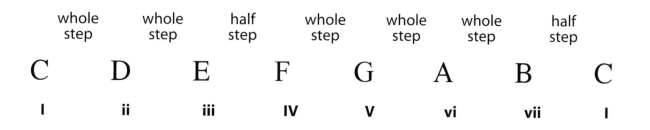

Chapter 4
Major & Minor Open Chords

Major Chords

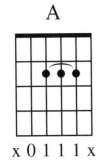
A
x 0 1 1 1 x

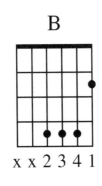
B
x x 2 3 4 1

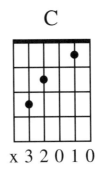
C
x 3 2 0 1 0

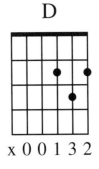
D
x 0 0 1 3 2

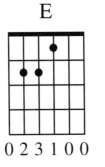
E
0 2 3 1 0 0

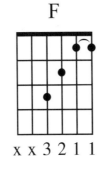
F
x x 3 2 1 1

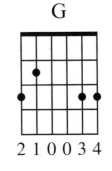
G
2 1 0 0 3 4

Minor Chords

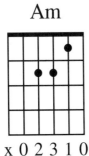
Am
x 0 2 3 1 0

Bm
x x 3 4 2 1

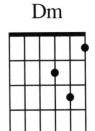
Cm
3fr
x x 3 4 2 1

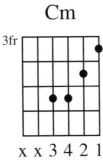
Dm
x 0 0 2 3 1

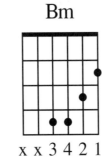
Em
0 2 3 0 0 0

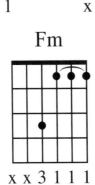
Fm
x x 3 1 1 1

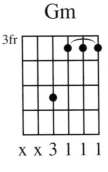
Gm
3fr
x x 3 1 1 1

Finger Exercise #2

Let's continue with a warm up exercise in tablature that will build coordination and strengthen your left hand. Fret each note individually using one finger at a time. Play each measure four times, then proceed to the next measure without pausing. This will help build endurance. Use alternate picking, and practice this exercise using the metronome for timing and control. Start out slowly and build speed gradually by slightly increasing the metronome setting each day.

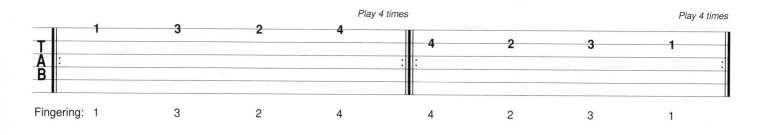

Fingering: 1   3   2   4   4   2   3   1

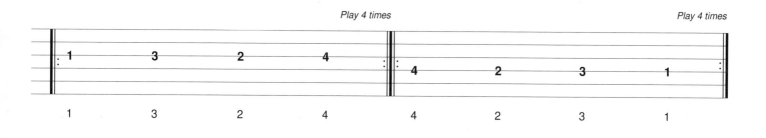

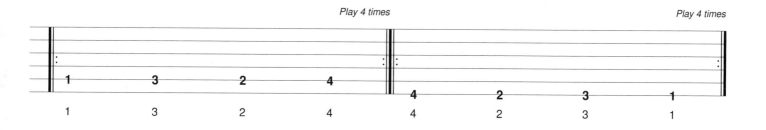

Minor Pentatonic Scales

In Chapter 2 we covered the first two positions of the A minor pentatonic scale. In this section, we'll go through the E minor pentatonic scale. E and A are two of the most popular keys used in rock and blues. All five positions are shown here in tab. To the right of each tab staff is a scale diagram. The root notes (all of the Es) have been circled on the staffs for your reference. When playing solos, pay attention to where the root notes are. The root notes should be considered home; you will constantly be returning to the root notes when constructing melodies.

Compare the fingerings for the 1st and 2nd positions of the E minor pentatonic scale to the 1st and 2nd positions of the A minor pentatonic scale from Chapter 2 and notice the similarities. All of these scale positions can be played in other keys by moving the entire pattern to a different fret.

1st Position E Minor Pentatonic Scale (open)

1st position
(open)

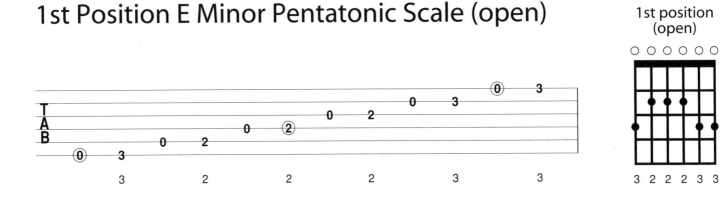

2nd Position E Minor Pentatonic Scale

2nd position

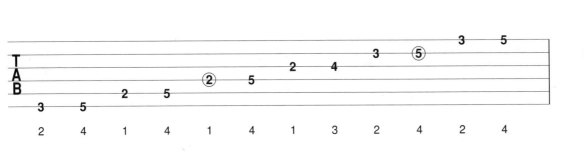

3rd Position E Minor Pentatonic Scale

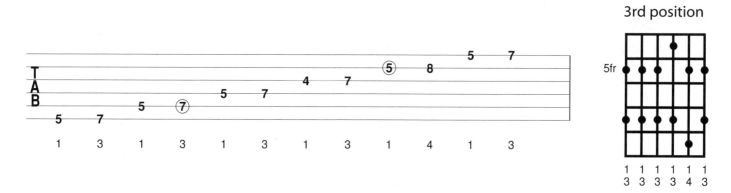

4th Position E Minor Pentatonic Scale

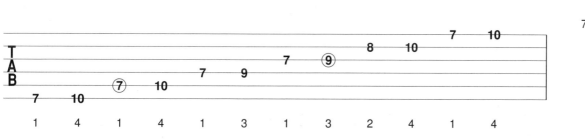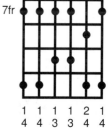

5th Position E Minor Pentatonic Scale

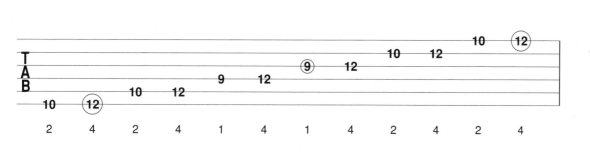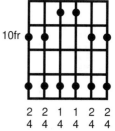

1st Position E Minor Pentatonic Scale (12th fret)

The first position of the Em pentatonic scale can also be transposed one octave higher and played in closed position at the 12th fret. To play any scale position an octave higher or lower, move the scale pattern 12 frets in the appropriate direction.

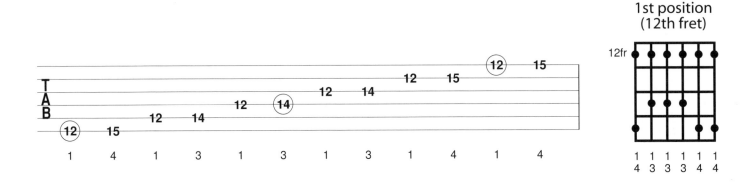

The E Minor Pentatonic Scale Fretboard Diagram

Once you have all five positions of the minor pentatonic scales mastered, you'll be able to play solos in any position on the neck. Remember that there are only five different name notes in the scale, and the different positions are just groupings of these same notes in different octaves and different places on the neck. The 1st and 2nd positions in this key can also be transposed one octave higher and are shown below in the fretboard diagram. Notice how each position overlaps the next; the left side of one position is the right side of the next one and so on. Think of these scale positions as building blocks (like Legos). When soloing, you can move from position to position and play across the entire fretboard.

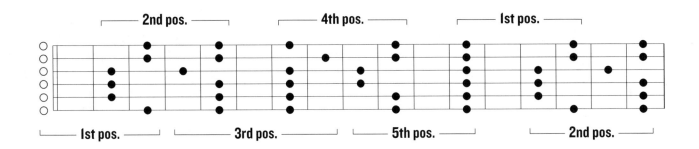

Blues Rhythm #2

The following rhythm is a standard I - IV - V progression in E with a shuffle feel. Listen to the backing track at www.rockhousemethod.com to get the proper feel and play along with the band. Pay attention to the strumming directions above the bottom staff and follow the instructor on the CD for tips on how to get the proper strumming motion. This is a popular blues riff that's used in many blues songs at different tempos. Memorize the rhythm, download the backing track and play along until you've got it down.

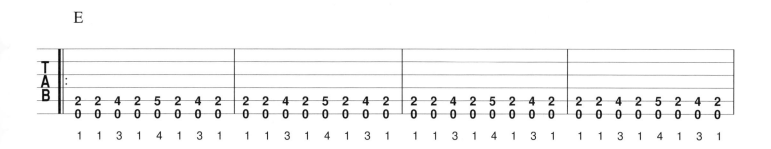

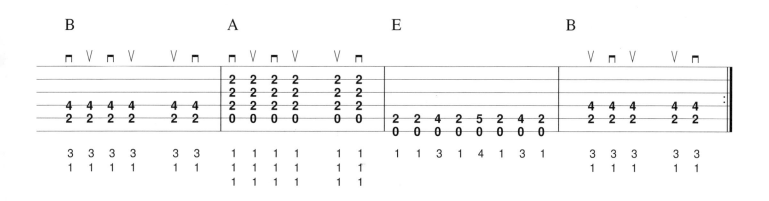

53

Advanced Lead Techniques

Half Step Bends

To play a half step bend, only bend the note slightly until is is one half step higher (the same pitch as one fret higher on the guitar). To perform a bend and release, first bend the note up and then release the note back to its original pitch without picking the string again. The release is indicated by a downward arrow pointing to the tab number in parentheses.

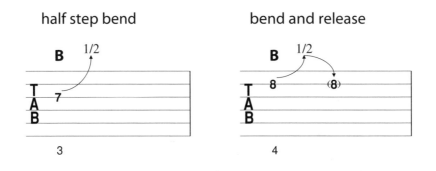

Here are some more examples of first, third and fourth finger half step bends in the context of a lead using the 1st position A minor pentatonic scale. Try playing in different positions, incorporating all of the bending techniques.

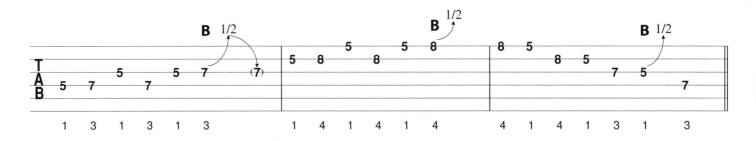

Hammer Ons and Pull Offs

The following exercise contains hammer ons and pull offs in combination. The slurs encompass three notes, so only pick the first one. Hammer on for the second note, then pull off to the third note.

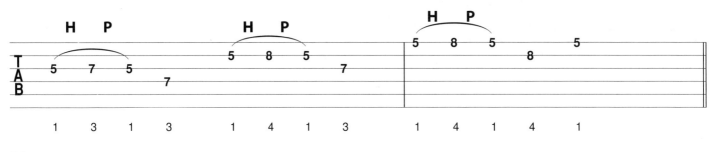

Slides

In the following example, slide from note to note without lifting your finger off the fretboard. The "S" above the staff indicates a slide and the line between the notes shows the direction of the slide (up or down the neck). If there is a slur connecting two or more notes, pick only the first note and slide directly to the next without picking. You can perform slides using any finger, but you'll probably use first and third finger slides more often. This exercise is played using the notes of the first position A minor pentatonic scale. After you get this down, try using the slide technique in other positions as well.

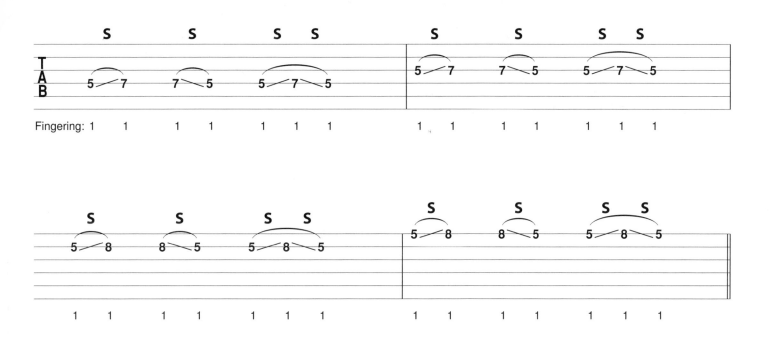

Vibrato

Vibrato is the small, fast shaking of a note. Vibrato is indicated by a squiggly line above the staff, extending out from above a note. While sustaining a note, shake your finger slightly and "dig in" to the note to slightly vibrate the pitch and give it more expression. Vibrato can also be applied while bending.

Complete Blues Lead

The following blues lead in the key of E uses the E minor pentatonic scales and contains examples of bends, hammer ons and pull offs. This lead can be played over the Blues Rhythm #2 from earlier in this section, as well as any other I - IV - V blues progression in E. The chord names are shown above the staff as a reference. Once you've gone through it step by step with the CD, try playing along with the backing track and adding your own personality to the bends and other techniques.

The first part of the solo begins in the 1st position scale at the 12th fret. After the first four measures, there are riffs in various other positions on the neck. The last section is a chromatic riff that's an example of a *blues turnaround* (a riff that brings you back around to the beginning of the progression).

This lead is designed to give you an idea of how to use the minor pentatonics, lead techniques and turnarounds in various positions on the fretboard. Once you're comfortable with this example, get creative and try coming up with your own solos.

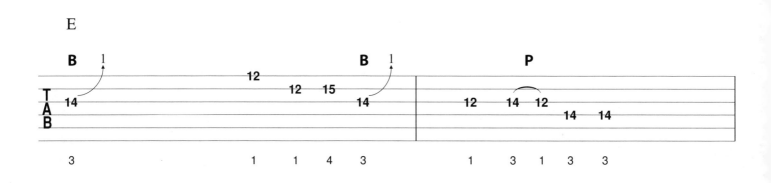

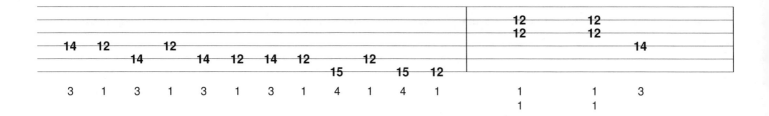

A

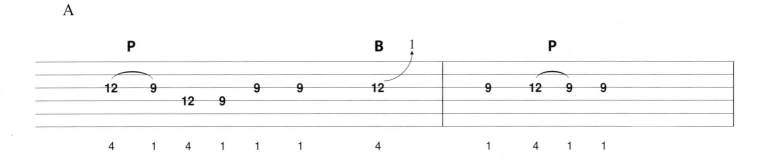

E

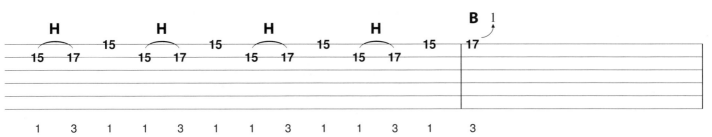

B   A

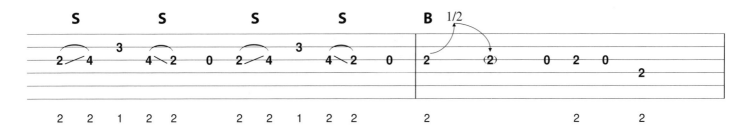

E   B

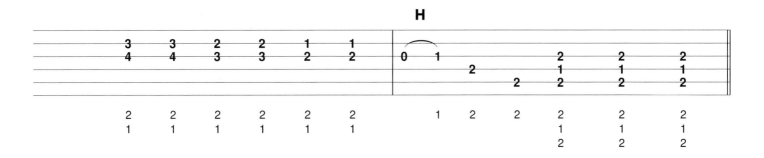

Hammer On & Pull Off Lead Pattern

The following lead pattern exercise is played in the 1st position E minor pentatonic scale and has been designed to show you some new ways to use hammer ons and pull offs when playing solos. Listen to the CD to learn the proper rhythmic phrasing. Memorize the patterns and gradually speed up the tempo of the metronome. Practice playing the pattern in all five positions of the scale.

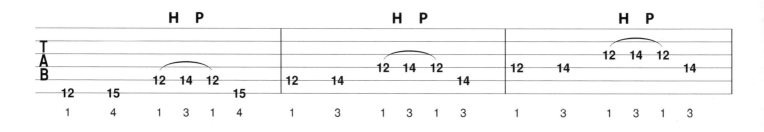

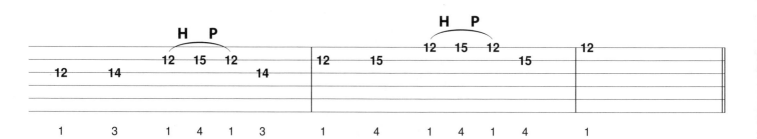

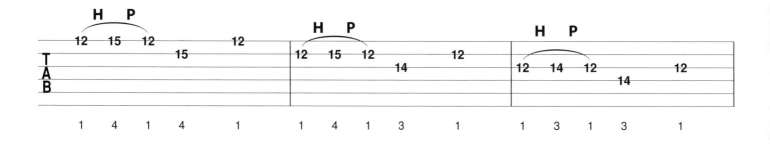

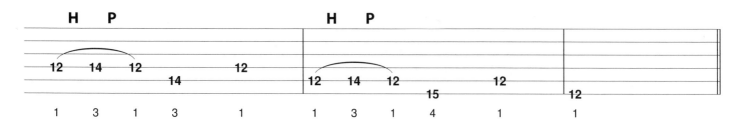

Five Position Lead Pattern

This lead pattern uses the A minor pentatonic scale and is played across all five positions of the scale. The fingerings are suggested fingerings; notice that the fingerings differ on the ascending and descending patterns. This exercise demonstrates various ways to switch from position to position. Play through the entire example along with the metronome and start out slowly until you're comfortable with the position changes.

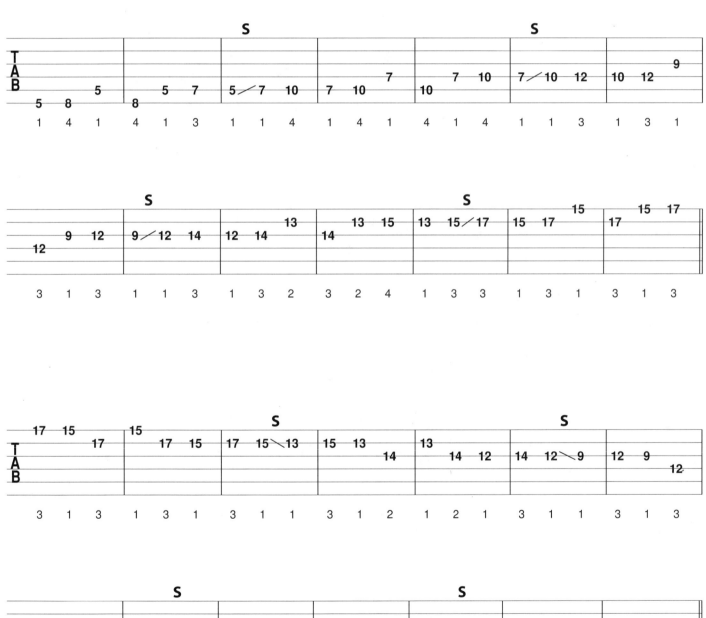

Sixteenth Note Scale Pattern

Sixteenth notes are four notes played within one beat. Sixteenth notes can be counted as groups of four notes: "one, two, three, four, one, two, three, four." You can also count sixteenth notes as "one-e-and-a, two-e-and-a," to help keep track of what number beat you are on. The following sixteenth note scale pattern ascends and descends through the 1st position of the C major scale in groups of four notes; the barlines have been placed after each grouping for reading convenience and the left hand fingering is indicated below the tab staff. Practice slowly with a metronome and gradually build up speed, remembering to use consistent, alternate picking.

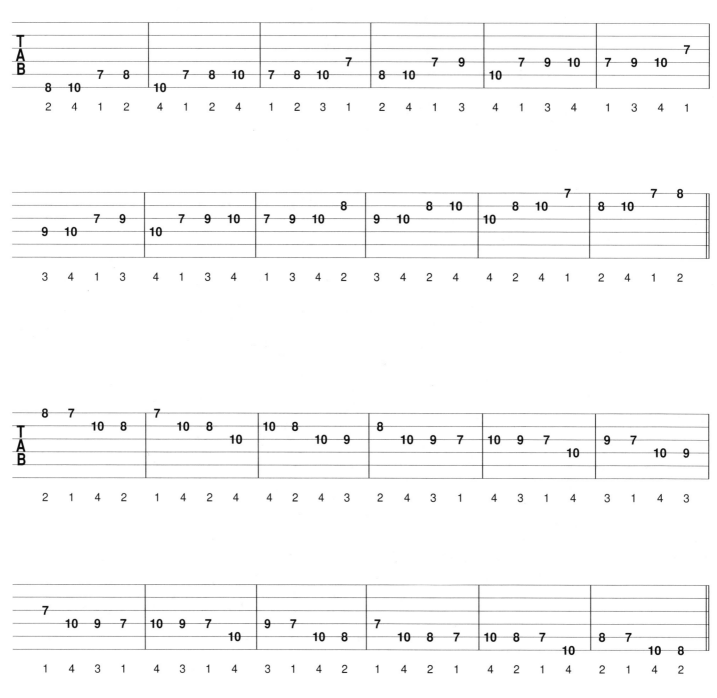

60

Putting It All Together

Complete Song Rhythm & Lead

For the last part of this chapter we'll learn a complete song rhythm, then show you how to use all of the different lead techniques to play solos over it. Follow along with the CD or download the bass and drum backing track from the Lesson Support Site and play along with the band. This rhythm is in the key of Em, so you can use every position of the E minor pentatonic scale to play solos over it.

This rock progression incorporates dead strums, performed by muting the strings with your left hand and strumming the muted strings. These muted notes are shown using Xs on the tab staff below. Pay attention to the picking symbols; they show you when to upstrum or downstrum. This particular example places dead strums between normal strums of the Em chord, giving the progression more of a percussive sound and a rock feel. The muted strums can be performed by slightly lifting your left hand fingers while still touching the strings with them.

The first measure starts with an Em barre chord and goes to a D major barre chord. This change is repeated three times before switching to a C chord and riff in the last measure. The riff uses a slide, hammer on and pull off; all of the notes that are struck should be downpicked. The fingering for the riff is shown underneath the staff.

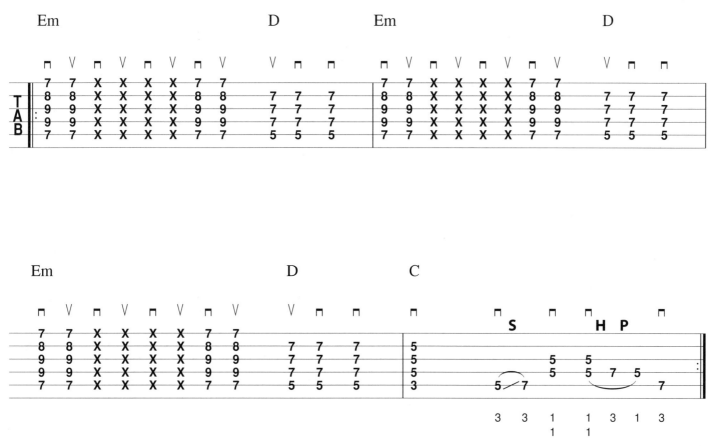

The following example is the first part of the lead performed on the CD for this section. It incorporates all of the techniques we've covered in the book using various positions of the E minor pentatonic scales. This solo has been tabbed out here to get you started and show you how it's done. The point of this lesson is for you to understand how to improvise, so don't get caught up in trying to learn this note for note. Instead, take a quick look through these riffs and spend more time creating your own.

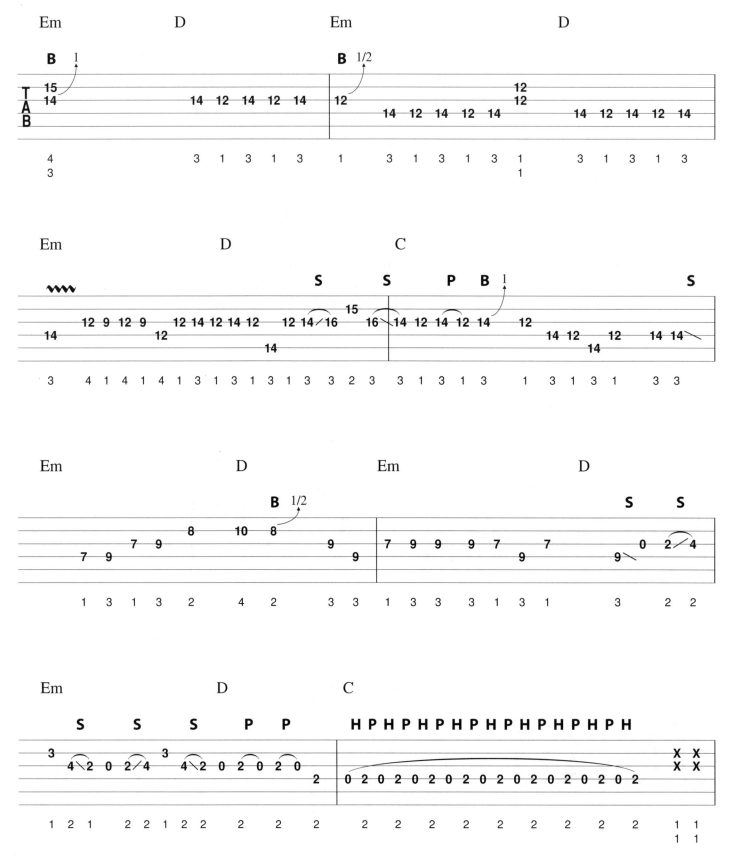

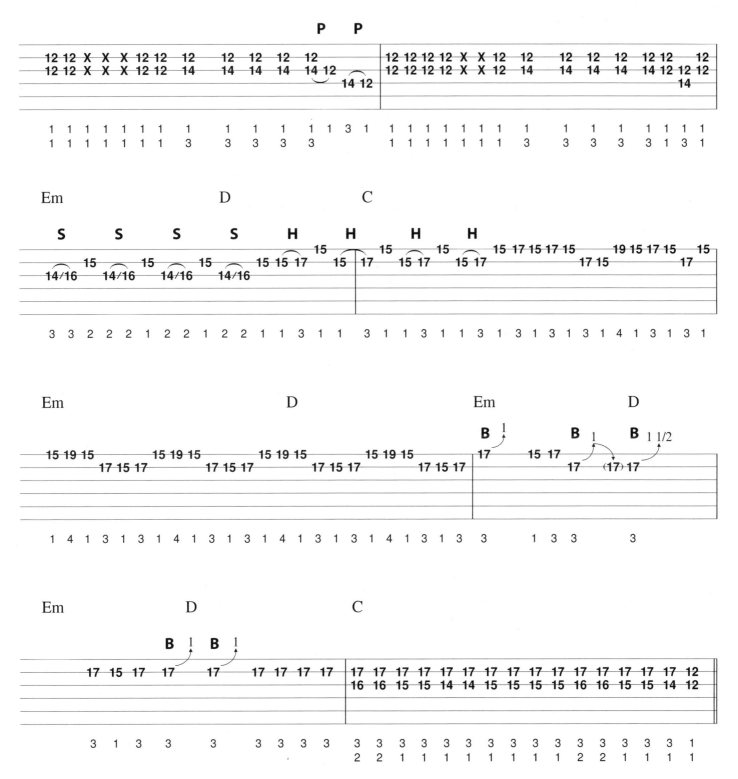

end of chapter 4

Before you continue to the next section, use your member number and log on to www.rockhousemethod.com to visit our online community. Review the additional information, take a quiz and test your knowledge of power chords, barre chords, advanced lead techniques, major scales and theory. Download the many backing tracks available online and jam along with the rock house instructors!

Chapter 5
Natural Minor Scales

Many modern Rock and Blues players have incorporated the use of full natural minor scales into their soloing. The pentatonic scales you've already learned are abbreviated versions of the regular major and minor scales. The pentatonic scales contain five notes; the natural minor scale contains seven notes. The word "natural" refers to the fact that the scale is in its original unaltered state. The A natural minor scale is particularly unique because this key contains all natural notes (no sharp or flat notes). The notes in an A natural minor scale are A - B - C - D - E - F - G. The natural minor scale can be used to create more complex and interesting melodies.

Below are the five basic positions of the A natural minor scale shown ascending and descending. The root notes have all been circled on the staff and scale diagrams.

1st Position A Minor Scale

1st position

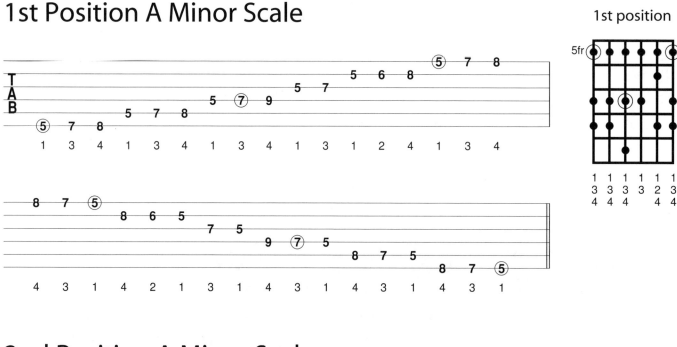

2nd Position A Minor Scale

2nd position

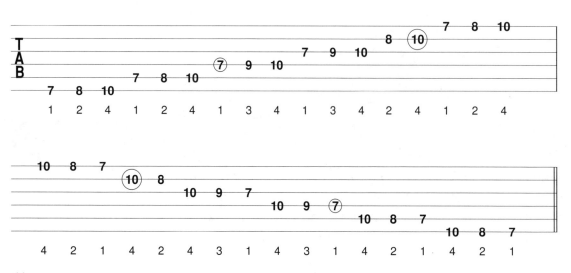

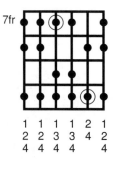

3rd Position A Minor Scale

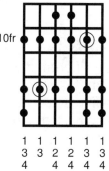

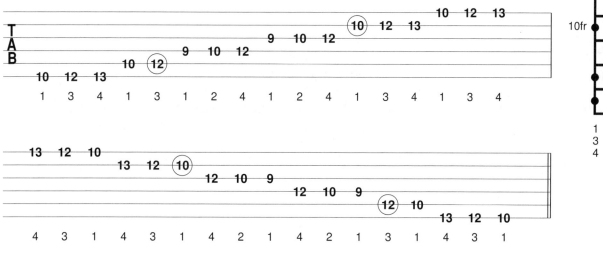

4th Position A Minor Scale

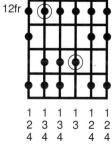

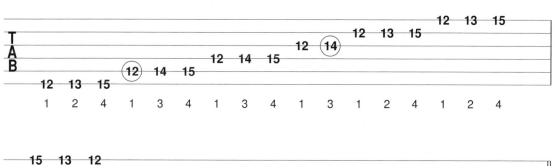

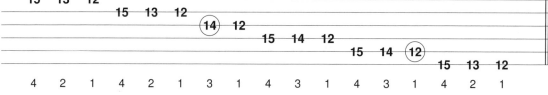

5th Position A Minor Scale

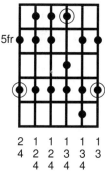

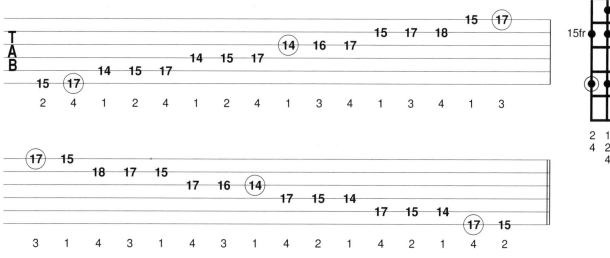

Arpeggios

An arpeggio is defined as the notes of a chord played separately. Major and minor arpeggios contain three different name notes: the *root note* (which is the same note as the arpeggio or chord's letter name), the *third* (which is the third scale step and letter name up from the root note), and the *fifth* (the fifth scale step and letter name up from the root note). Full major and minor chords on the guitar are actually groups of root notes, thirds and fifths in different octaves that your hand can reach within that position. Once you know the theory behind which individual notes belong in the chord and where they are on the fretboard, you can create your own chords. More information on arpeggio and chord theory can be found at www.rockhousemethod.com and in the Learn Rock Guitar Advanced program.

Major Arpeggio

The following examples are two octave A major arpeggios. In the first example, follow the picking symbols and use normal, consistent alternate picking.

Alternate Picking

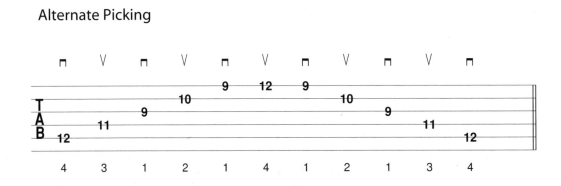

Now try the same A major arpeggio using the *sweep picking* technique. Sweep picking is performed by dragging the pick across the strings in one smooth, flowing motion. In the example below, sweep downward with the pick across the ascending part of the arpeggio. Play the three notes on the 1st string using a combination hammer on and pull off and then sweep back up across the strings with the pick using the same smooth motion. Sweep picking is a very useful technique for playing fast arpeggio runs. The downward sweep picking motion is also referred to as *raking*. This technique may be indicated in music and tablature using the word "rake" followed by a dashed line.

Sweep Picking

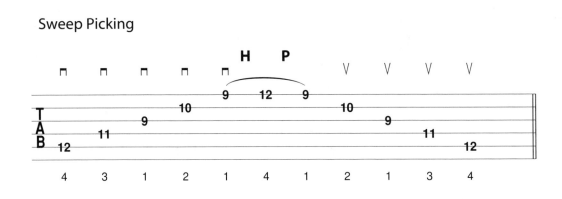

Minor Arpeggio

Here are the A minor arpeggios using alternate picking and sweep picking. Just like with full chords, major arpeggios have a happy or bright tone, while minor arpeggios have a sad or melancholy tone.

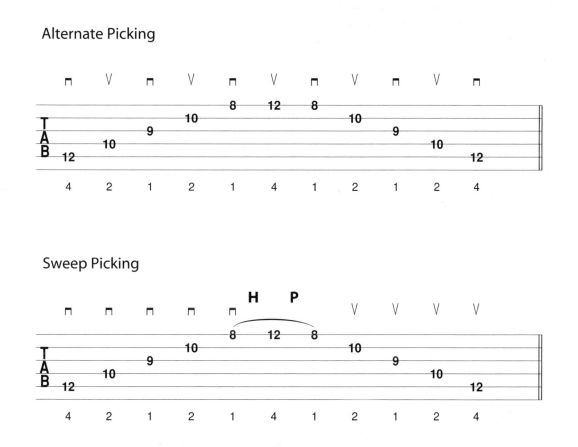

Notice there is only a small difference between the major and minor arpeggios. All of the thirds in the minor arpeggios are one fret (or one half step) lower than the thirds in the major arpeggio. This slight difference is what makes a chord or an arpeggio either major or minor. These notes are also referred to as *major thirds* or *minor thirds*. The staff below shows all of the note names and the placement of the major and minor thirds in the two octave arpeggios.

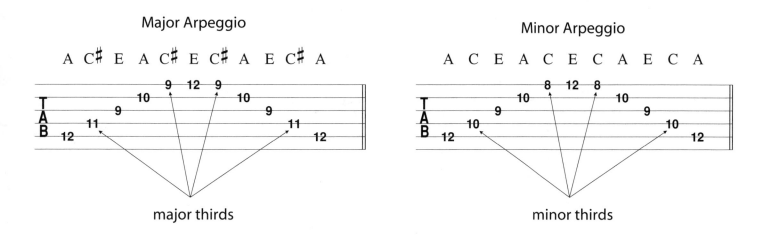

Arpeggios - Small Three String Sweeps

The sweeping motion in this exercise is performed by the picking hand. Sweep across the strings with the pick in a down-down then up-up motion followed by a hammer on and pull off combination. This is a standard lead technique used for playing fast arpeggios in metal solos. Play through the example slowly at first to get the sweeping motion down, then play in time to the metronome and gradually build up speed.

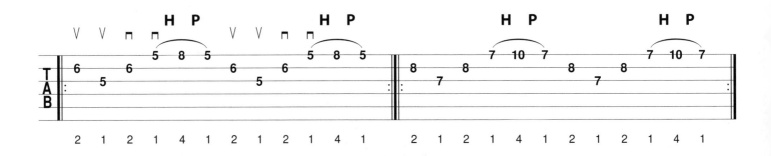

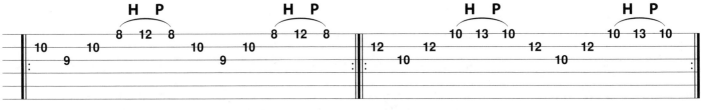

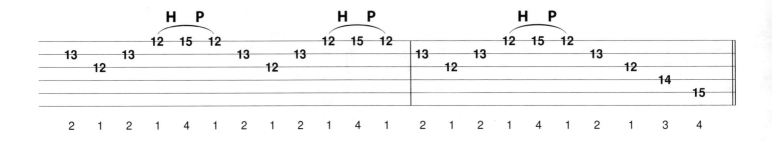

Bi-Dextral Hammer Ons

This technique introduces the right hand tap, which requires you to reach over to the neck with your right hand and hammer on the note using your right hand index or middle finger. After tapping the note, pull off with your right hand finger to the lower notes on the neck that should be fretted with your left hand fingers. The "R" above the tab staff indicates a right hand tap. This technique allows you to hammer on and pull off full arpeggios and other wide interval phrases very quickly.

If you tap with your middle finger, you can keep the pick in position in your hand. If you feel more comfortable tapping with your index finger, you can use a technique called "palming the pick" where you tuck the pick under your middle finger to get it out of the way. After playing the riff, bring it back into position to go back to regular picking.

The following riff is an example of what you can do with bi-dextral hammer ons. Once you're comfortable with the technique, experiment with it at different frets and on different strings. You can also do other fun things with this technique, such as bending a note in your left hand and then tapping a note above it while holding the bend. This bend and tap technique was made popular by Billy Gibbons.

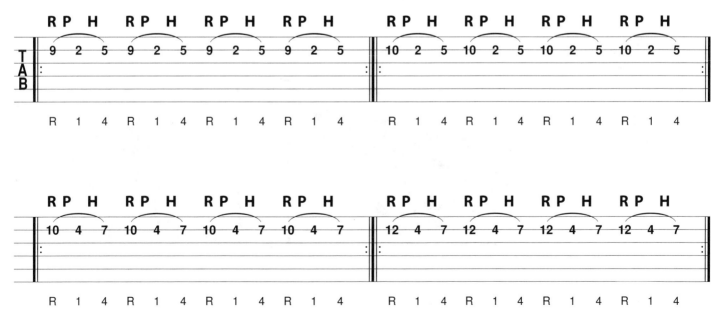

Full Form Chords

The following full form chords are extensions of the regular major and minor chords. The major 7th (maj7) and minor 7th (m7) chords are commonly used to achieve a fuller, jazzier sound. These full form chords are *moveable chords* since they contain no open strings. Notice that the lowest note of each chord is the root note of the chord; you can move the chords to any fret along the 5th or 6th strings and transpose them to any other key. To transpose these chords, you can refer to the chart from Lesson 2.

In the Gmaj7 chord, mute the 5th string using the arch of your first finger on your left hand. Use the same technique to deaden the muted inner strings in the Cm7 and Bm7♭5 chords as well.

Gmaj7

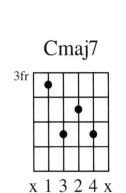

1 x 3 4 2 x

```
T    3
A    4
     4
B    3
```

Cmaj7

3fr

x 1 3 2 4 x

```
T    5
A    4
     5
B    3
```

70

Gm7

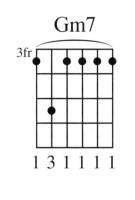

3fr

1 3 1 1 1 1

```
T  3
A  3
   3
   3
   5
B  3
```

Cm7

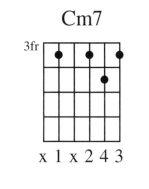

3fr

x 1 x 2 4 3

```
   3
T  4
A  3
B  3
```

Bm7♭5

x 2 x 3 4 1

```
   1
T  3
A  2
B  2
```

Chord Theory

Now that you've learned a little scale theory and know the full form chords, we can expand on those principles and explore the major scale chord formula. Chord theory is easier to understand in terms of musical notes, so for this section we'll use some very basic music notation. It's also a good idea for musicians of any level to have some understanding of the concepts of written music. Below is the C major scale shown using traditional musical notes. The letters above the staff show which note is which. In regular music notation the notes are written on lines or spaces. As you count up through the musical alphabet, the notes on the staff progress upward in a line-space-line-space order.

Chords are made up of several notes played together using a combination of specific intervals. For simple major and minor chords, the intervals used are the root note, third and fifth. Simply choose a root note and count up to the third and fifth notes above it in the scale, and that will give you the three notes in the chord.

Using just the natural notes in the key of C (without using any sharps or flats), we can build a chord above every step of the C major scale. Each step will be the root note of a different chord, then just add the thirds and fifths above each of these scale steps. As before, this formula holds true for all major keys. The combination of intervals within a chord (the exact distance in pitch between the notes) is what determines if a chord is major or minor. In a major chord, the distance between the root note and the third is two whole steps (also called a *major third*). In a minor chord, the distance between the root note and the third is only one and a half steps (also called a *minor third*). The exception is the diminished chord, indicated with the small superscript "o" in the chord name. Diminished chords contain a minor third as well as a flatted fifth.

The staffs below show the major, minor and diminished chords in the key of C major, and which scale steps they occur on. The I, IV and V chords are all major, while the ii, iii and vi chords are minor, and the vii chord is diminished. The upper and lower case Roman numerals reflect whether the chords are major or minor and diminished.

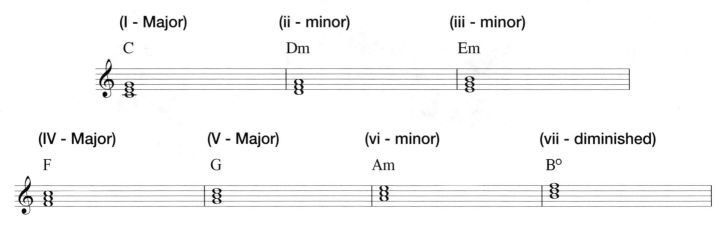

72

We can extend the C major scale chord formula to include the seventh above each root note as well, giving us the full form chords from the previous lesson. The full combination of the thirds, fifths and sevenths determine what type of chord occurs on each scale step. Familiarize yourself with all of the names and chord symbols used on the staffs below. This is the full C major scale chord formula. Remember that the placement of the intervals within a major scale is a natural musical phenomena, and this formula holds true for all the major keys.

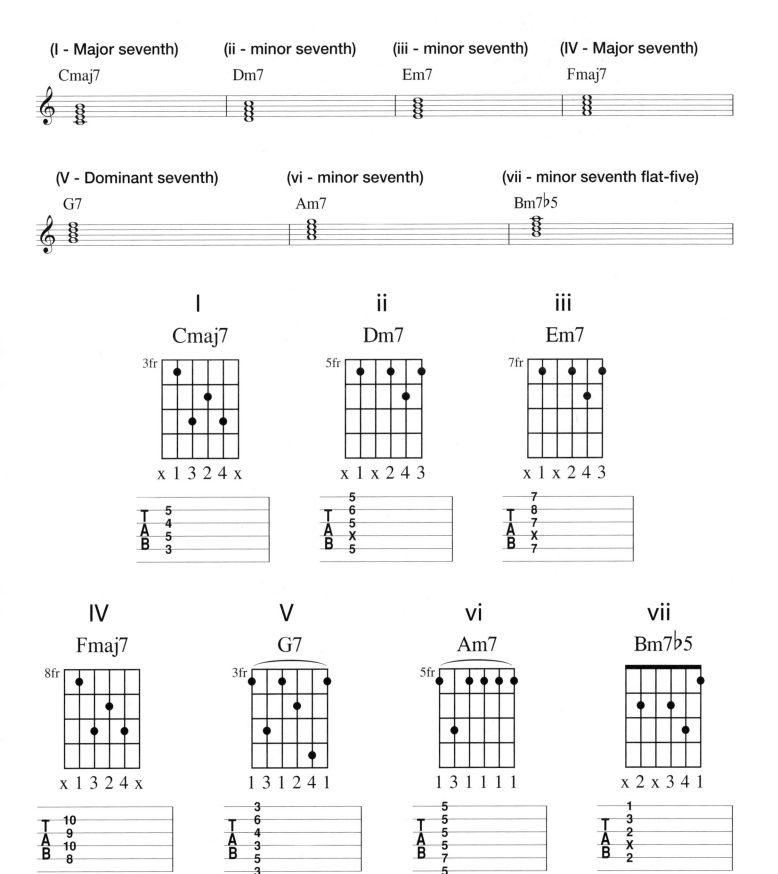

Progression Using the Circle of Fourths

The following progression is a slow blues in the key of Am. The rhythm is counted in three's and each chord is *arpeggiated* (the notes of each chord are picked out separately). Finger and hold the chord in each measure and let its notes ring out together. Follow the finger numbers under the tab staff to show you the proper chord fingerings. Play along with the backing track and practice the rhythm's slow ballad feel. The chord change progresses in a pattern of fourths; the distance from one chord to the next is the interval of a fourth. This is a common change that is also used in many musical styles ranging from classical to metal.

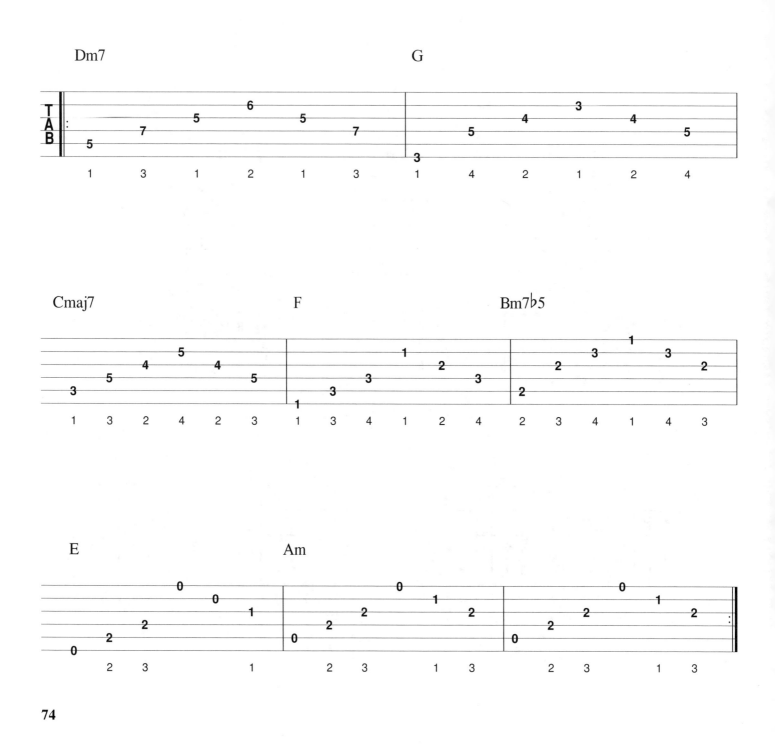

Melodic Lead

You can play leads over the previous Circle of Fourths progression using these scales. Here is an example lead that was improvised during this lesson on the CD. Play through the tab to get some ideas, then try creating your own leads.

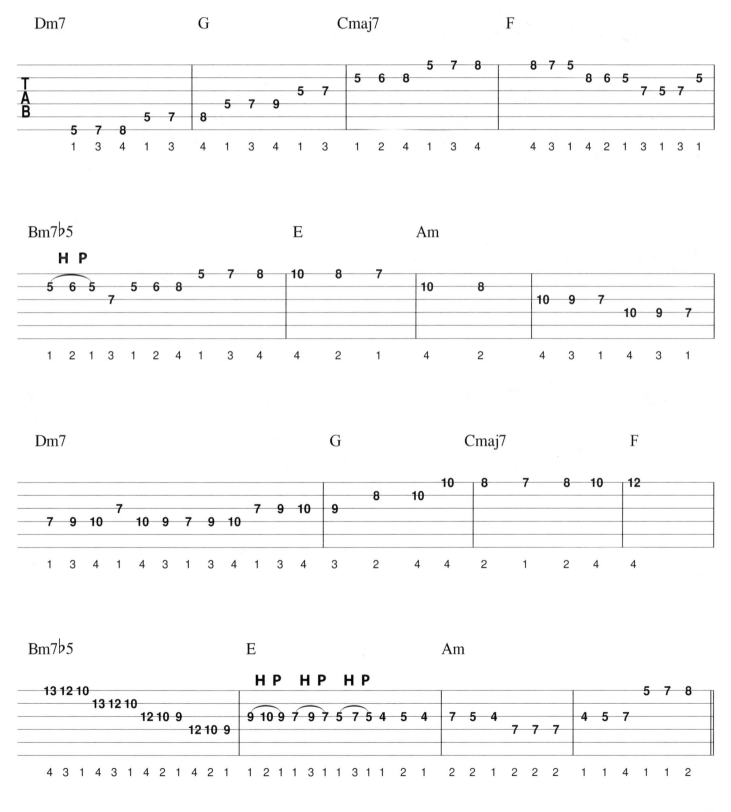

Workout Section

This invaluable bonus section contains a wide variety of exercises that target all areas of left and right hand technique. Get a good workout with these examples daily and you'll be on your way to mastering the guitar. Practice all of these examples with a metronome, advanced the tempos slightly every day.

Picking Exercise

This exercise is designed to strengthen your picking hand and increase coordination and control of the pick. Practice this exercise using all open strings; you don't need your left hand for this one at all. Follow the picking symbols to get the pattern correct. Repeat each measure for 30 seconds, then repeat the entire exercise for a full six minutes. You can practice this anytime, even while relaxing and watching TV.

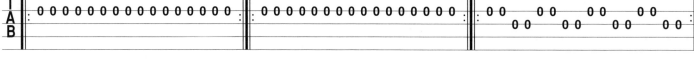

Open String Orchestration

This exercise uses very fast alternate picking. Keep the picking motion steady and in time. The entire exercise is played on one string, alternating between the open string and each fretted note. You can try this exercise on all six strings in different places along the fretboard.

```
  8  0  5  0  7  0  8  0  8  0  5  0  7  0  8  0 |10  0  7  0  8  0 10  0 10  0  7  0  8  0 10  0
T
A
B

  4     1     3     4     4     1     3     4     4     1     2     4     4     1     2     4
```

```
 12  0  8  0 10  0 12  0 12  0  8  0 10  0 12  0 |13  0 10  0 12  0 13  0 13  0 10  0 12  0 13  0
T
A
B

  4     1     3     4     4     1     3     4     4     1     3     4     4     1     3     4
```

Pinky Pull Off

This is an important exercise specifically crafted to develop your fourth finger. The fourth finger is usually your weakest and hardest to develop. Playing this exercise stretches out your hand and makes you use your pinky to reach for the notes. Keep your first finger barred across the first two strings at the 10th fret and leave it there while stretching up for the higher notes with your pinky. This hammer on and pull off pattern is especially useful when playing arpeggios.

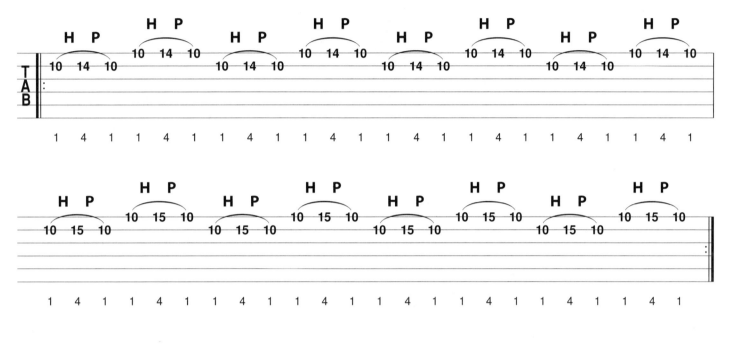

One Hand Rolls

42
disc 2

Here's an exercise designed to strengthen your left hand using a series of hammer ons and pull offs. All of the notes should be produced by the left hand only; don't use the pick at all. Your right hand can be used to mute the other strings.

Finger Frenzy

This is a finger exercise in tablature that will build coordination and strengthen your left hand. Fret each note individually, using one finger at a time. Play through each measure, proceeding to the next measure without pausing. This will help build endurance. Use alternate picking and practice this exercise using the metronome for timing and control.

```
T|--12--13--12--13--12--13--12--13--12--13--12--13--12--13--12--13--|
A|------------------------------------------------------------------|
B|------------------------------------------------------------------|
    1   2   1   2   1   2   1   2   1   2   1   2   1   2   1   2
```

```
--13--14--13--14--13--14--13--14--13--14--13--14--13--14--13--14--
------------------------------------------------------------------
    2   3   2   3   2   3   2   3   2   3   2   3   2   3   2   3
```

```
--14--15--14--15--14--15--14--15--14--15--14--15--14--15--14--15--
------------------------------------------------------------------
    3   4   3   4   3   4   3   4   3   4   3   4   3   4   3   4
```

```
--13--15--13--15--13--15--13--15--13--15--13--15--13--15--13--15--
------------------------------------------------------------------
    2   4   2   4   2   4   2   4   2   4   2   4   2   4   2   4
```

```
--12--15--12--15--12--15--12--15--12--15--12--15--12--15--12--15--
------------------------------------------------------------------
    1   4   1   4   1   4   1   4   1   4   1   4   1   4   1   4
```

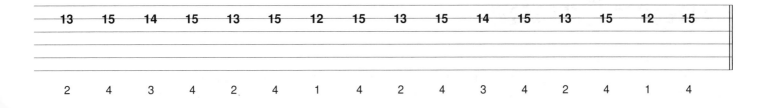

The Killer!!

This exercise is designed to work on your left hand coordination. Use consistent alternate picking throughout. Play through the first measure slowly until you memorize the pattern. Notice that all four fingers of the left hand are used in succession. For each consecutive measure, the pattern moves down one string. The bottom two tab staffs show the pattern in reverse.

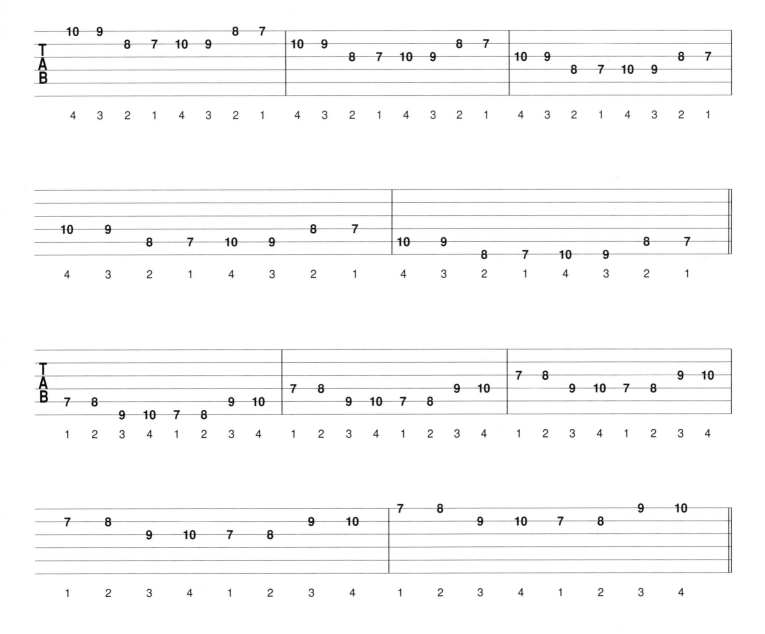

Finger Crusher

The finger crusher is a left hand workout that will make your fingers stronger and faster. Each section of the exercise starts with a two string pattern from the minor pentatonic scale. Play it four times in position, then move the pattern chromatically up the neck to the 12th fret and chromatically back down to where you started at the 5th fret.

Your hand will probably get sore and tired before you're even halfway through the exercise, but that just means you're doing it right and getting a great workout. Try to keep time with the metronome and make it your goal to get through the entire exercise without stopping.

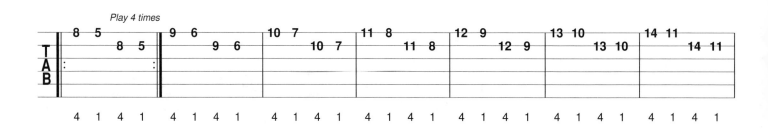

80

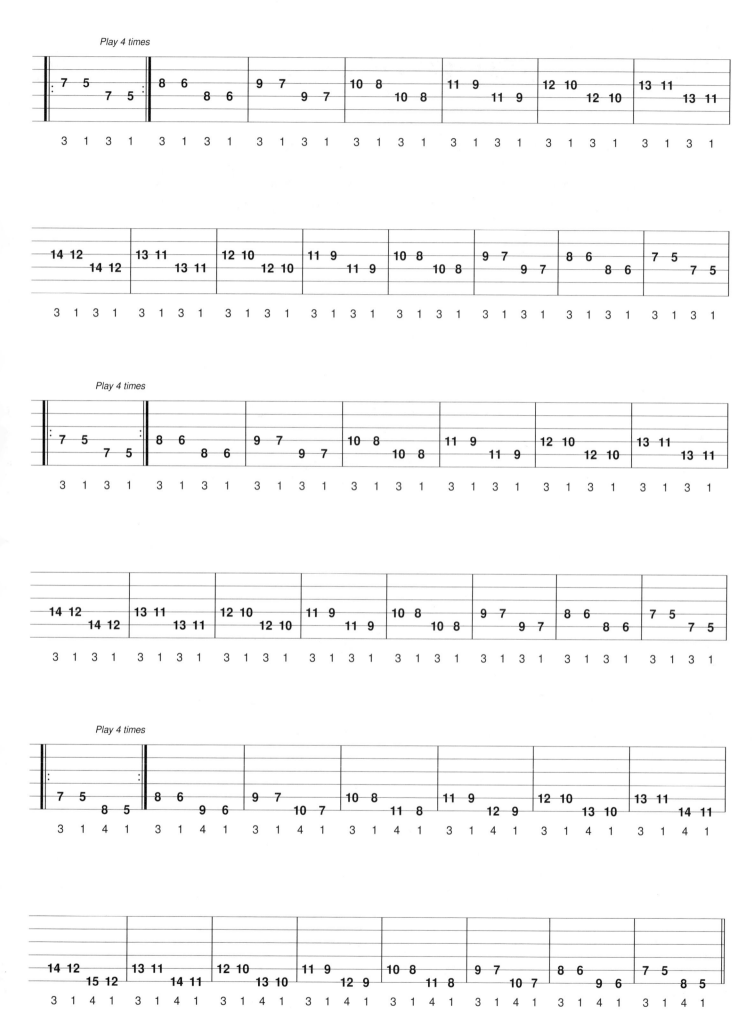

81

Johnny Blues

*Here's the first part of the inspirational piece "Johnny Blues" from my CD, **Drive**. This is a perfect example of how some of the best melodies can be suprisingly easy to play. The audio for this section is available on the included CD. You can also download this track as well as other songs from **Drive** at www.rockhousemethod.com.*

- John McCarthy

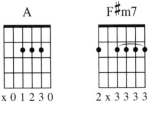

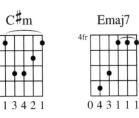
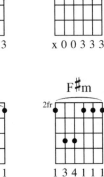
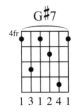

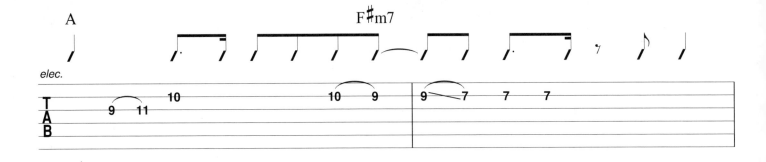

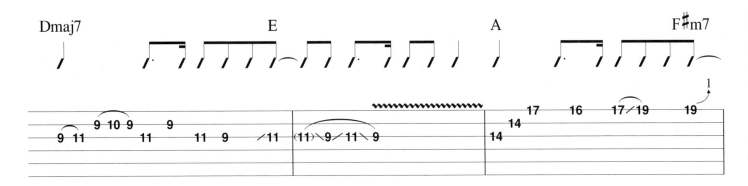

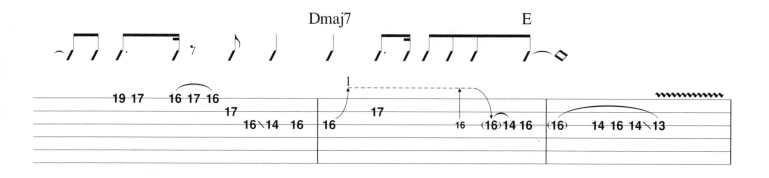

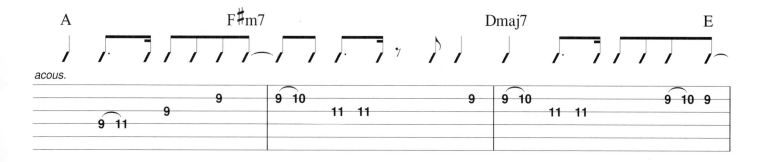

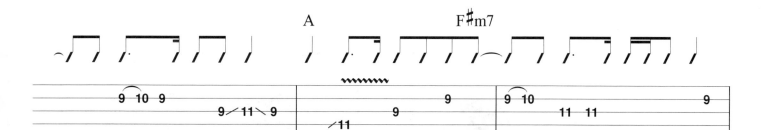

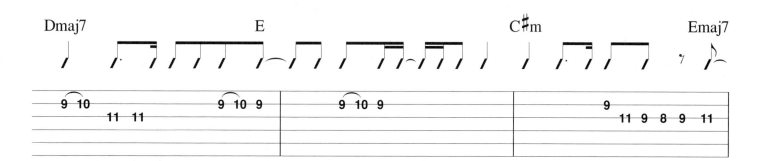

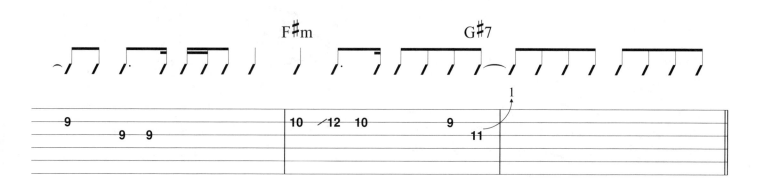

Changing a String

Old guitar strings may break or lose their tone and become harder to keep in tune. You might feel comfortable at first having a teacher or someone at a music store change your strings for you, but eventually you will need to know how to do it yourself. Changing the strings on a guitar is not as difficult as it may seem and the best way to learn how to do this is by practicing. Guitar strings are fairly inexpensive and you may have to go through a few to get it right the first time you try to restring your guitar. How often you change your strings depends entirely on how much you play your guitar, but if the same strings have been on it for months, it's probably time for a new set.

Most strings attach at the headstock in the same way, however electric and acoustic guitars vary in the way in which the string is attached at the bridge. Before removing the old string from the guitar, examine the way it is attached to the guitar and try to duplicate that with the new string. Acoustic guitars may use removeable bridge pins that fasten the end of the string to the guitar by pushing it into the bridge and securing it there. On some electric guitars, the string may need to be threaded through a hole in the back of the body.

Follow the series of photos below for a basic description of how to change a string. Before trying it yourself, read through the quick tips for beginners on the following page.

Use a string winder to loosen the string.

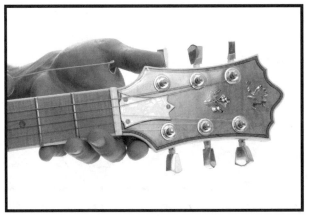

Remove the old string from the tuning post.

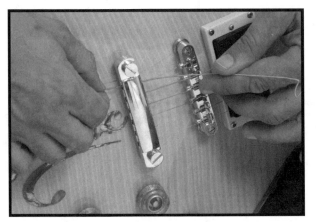

Pull the old string through the bridge and remove it from the guitar.

Remove the new string from the packaging and uncoil it.

Thread the end of the new string through the bridge.

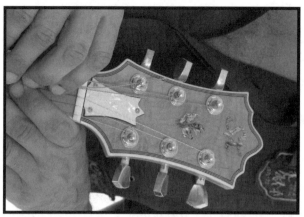

Pull the string along the neck and thread it through the small hole on the tuning post.

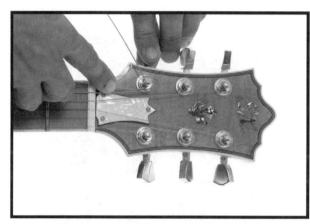

Hold the string in place just after the nut with your finger and tighten up the slack in the string with the machine head.

Carefully tighten the string and tune it to the proper pitch.

You can cut the old string off the guitar but you may want to unwind it instead and save it as a spare in case you break a string later.

Check to make sure you have the correct string in your hand before putting it on the guitar. The strings may be color coded at the end to help you identify them.

Be sure to wind the string around the tuning post in the proper direction (see photos), and leave enough slack to wind the string around the post several times. The string should wind around the post underneath itself to form a nice, neat coil.

Once the extra slack is taken up and the string is taught, tune it very gradually to pitch, being careful not to overtighten and accidentally break the new string.

Once the string is on the guitar and tightened up, you can cut the excess string sticking out from the tuning post with a wire cutter. The sharp tail end that is left can be bent downward with the wire cutter to get it out of the way and avoid cutting or stabbing your finger on it.

Check the ends of the string to make sure it is sitting correctly on the proper saddle and space on the nut.

New strings will go out of tune very quickly until they are broken in. You can gently massage the new string with your thumbs and fingers once it's on the guitar, slightly stretching the string out and helping to break it in. Then retune the string and repeat this process a few times for each string.

Guitar Accessories

Strings & Picks

Strings and picks are both available in different gauges. Heavier gauge strings produce a thicker, fuller sound; lighter gauges are thinner, easier to bend, and great for soloing. There are many different types of picks in different thicknesses. A heavy pick may offer you more control for lead playing, but medium and light picks have a flexibility that's good for rhythm playing. A fingerpick is a type of ring that you wear on your thumb for downpicking, allowing all of your fingers to be available for more complex fingerpicking. When changing your strings, you'll probably want to use a string winder. A string winder is a simple gadget that fits right over the machine heads so that you can quickly wind or unwind a string.

Strings come in various styles and gauges.

Different types of picks are available.

String winders make changing strings easier.

Music Stands & Metronomes

As soon as you begin your first guitar lesson, you'll notice how important it is to have a music stand. Whenever you try to learn a new song from sheet music, or even go through a lesson in this book, you'll want to have the music right in front of you where it's close and easy to read. Don't try to balance a book on your lap or read it from the floor. If you're practicing scales and exercises or working out a difficult new guitar line, you can use a metronome to set a steady practice tempo and keep yourself in time. There are mechanical or electronic models, or you can download the free one from www.rockhousemethod.com and use your computer to keep time.

Capos & Slides

A capo is a moveable clamp that attaches to the neck of the guitar and barres across all six strings. Whichever fret the capo is placed at can then be thought of as the nut; the capo transposes the entire guitar to that position, making it possible to play all of the open chords there. Many acoustic players prefer the full open chord sound and use capos almost exclusively. Capos are popular at the 1st, 2nd, 3rd, 5th and 7th frets, but you can place a capo anywhere at all on the neck. A capo at the 12th fret transposes the guitar one octave higher and gives it a bright, mandolin tone.

An essential element of the blues guitar sound is the slide. A slide is a sleeve (usually glass) that fits over the ring finger of your left hand. With a slide you can slide notes or chords in a steady, smooth motion, making the guitar "talk." Slide guitar is also very popular in many rock styles, and can be heard in songs like "Freebird" and "Bad to the Bone."

Capo properly placed at the 2nd fret.

A slide can be worn on your ring finger.

Effects

Effects play an important role in every guitar player's arsenal. There are many different effects and different types of units available for you to experiment with while creating your own signature sounds. You can use foot pedals as well as rack mount effects units. Some basic effects that are useful are distortion, chorus, flangers and phasers, compressors, harmonizers and wah wah pedals.

With newer USB converters and software, you can also plug your guitar into a computer and play your way through cyberspace. Just connect right to your pc and you can get access to a whole arsenal of software featuring guitar effects, amp sounds, interactive lessons and virtual recording studios.

Various guitar effects pedals.

Tuners

An electronic tuner is a necessity for any gigging guitarist, and tuners have become so common that they're often included in other effects units. Tuners are also sometimes put right into a guitar's electronics. If you don't have a tuner, you can download the free online tuner at our support website.

Electronic digital tuner

Straps

Acoustic guitar straps can attach at the body if there's a strap button there. If not, a strap can be tied to the headstock between the nut and the machine heads. Straps come in a variety of materials and styles. When picking out a strap, try to find one that's both comfortable and that looks good with your guitar. Also available are strap locks (locking buttons that will keep the strap secured to the guitar).

Guitar straps

Cords

Investing a few dollars more to get a nice, heavy duty guitar cord is worthwhile. The cheaper ones don't last very long, while a professional quality cable can work perfectly for years. Some of the better cords even include a lifetime warranty. Cords also come in a variety of lengths, gauges and colors.

Guitar cords

Cases & Stands

The two main types of guitar cases are hardshell cases and softshell cases. Hardshell cases are more expensive and have a sturdy construction designed for maximum protection during travel. A much lighter and smaller alternative to the traditional guitar case is a gig bag: a padded, zippered guitar glove that is carried over the shoulders like a backpack. Guitar stands are usually collapsible and easy to take with you, but you can also use one at home to keep your guitar on display when you're not practicing.

Hardshell case

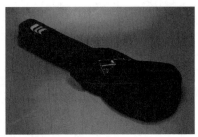
Gig bag

Make Your Own Tool Kit

Put together your own tool kit by keeping all of the important tools and spare parts you need in one place, like a small backpack or a compartment inside your guitar case. You should always have spare strings, a string winder, picks, batteries, and any small screwdrivers or wrenches that fit your guitar. You can purchase a multipurpose tool designed especially for guitarists (sort of like a pocket knife without the knife) that contains a few different types of screwdrivers and an assortment of allen wrenches. Some other good things to keep with you: wire cutters, fuses if your amp uses them, guitar polish and a soft cloth, music paper and pencil, and duct tape. You may also want to keep a small recording device handy to record your own musical ideas and use them to start writing your own songs.

A collection of important accessories.

Crossword Puzzle

Find the famous guitarists that played the songs listed below
Answers on page 93

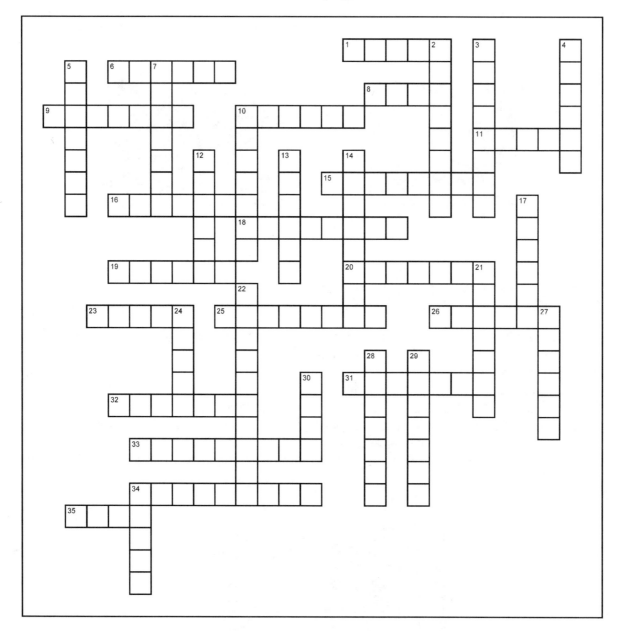

Across

1. WELCOME TO THE JUNGLE
6. LUCILLE
8. I LOVE ROCK AND ROLL
9. PURPLE HAZE
10. MORE THAN A FEELING
11. IRON MAN
15. ERUPTION
16. KILLING IN THE NAME OF
18. SATISFACTION
19. CAT SCRATCH FEVER
20. REBEL YELL
23. WALK THIS WAY
25. PEACE SELLS
26. FRANKENSTEIN
31. SURRENDER
32. CROSSFIRE
33. MY GENERATION
34. SMOKE ON THE WATER
35. STAIRWAY TO HEAVEN

Down

2. ENTER SANDMAN
3. SURFING WITH THE ALIEN
4. SMELLS LIKE TEEN SPIRIT
5. DETROIT ROCK CITY
7. LIGHT MY FIRE
10. LIVIN' ON A PRAYER
12. MAGIC MAN
13. SUGAR MAGNOLIA
14. TAXMAN
17. PURPLE RAIN
21. BLACK MAGIC WOMAN
22. GO YOUR OWN WAY
24. HIGHWAY TO HELL
27. CRAZY TRAIN
28. TUSH
29. LAYLA
30. KISS ME DEADLY
34. JOHNNY B. GOODE

Crossword Answer Key

CD Track List & Index

So Easy Electric Guitar - CD 1

BD = Bass and Drums on the track
BDR = Bass, Drums and Rhythm Guitar on the track
BDRL = Bass, Drums, Rhythm Guitar and Lead on the track

So Easy Electric Guitar - CD 2